Public Speaking WORKOUT

Exercise Your Body Parts

Your Public Speaking Workout: Exercise Your Body Parts

Published by
Funny Management Publishing
Boca Raton, Florida

All rights reserved. No part of this book may be reproduced or transmitted in any form or by any means, electronic or mechanical, including photocopying, recording or by any information storage and retrieval system without written permission from the authors, except for the inclusion of brief quotations in a review.

Copyright ©2000

ISBN: 0-9704301-0-8

Illustrations by
Jamie Blacksher

Cover Design by
John Windhorst, DOV Graphics

Art Production by
Michelle Frey, Tammy Norton
& Cathie Tibbetts, DOV Graphics

About the Authors

Dorothy Lynn and Jessica Selasky are a mother and daughter team and they rarely disagree because Jessica usually has just the right answers for everything. Of course, Dorothy raised her to be a good thinker. When they decided to write **Your Public Speaking Workout**, they wanted it to be a true collaboration, so they both contributed insights gained from their management and professional speaking experiences.

Dorothy has been in the training and development field since the mid-70s when she became the first female program director for The Presidents Association, a division of the American Management Associations. During her career, she has written another book on the subject of public speaking, **The Power of In-Person Communications**, with Charles Reilly. Her passion is to inspire and prepare as many people as possible to become confident and to experience non-stop confidence in everything they do. That's why she and Jessica are writing their new book, NON-STOP CONFIDENCE, which will be available in the fall of 2001.

Jessica began her management career with General Electric and then moved on to create and manage a large telecommunications center at FACS, a subsidiary of Federated Department Stores in Cincinnati. She is President of the Greater Cincinnati Chapter of ASTD, (American Society for Training and Development) and is on the Board of Directors of Joy, an outdoor educational facility. She has designed and delivered new and unusual management training programs including Signals of Communication and FUNNY management. Jessica finds the idea of sharing smiles and laughter irresistible as she helps people learn difficult concepts quickly and easily.

Dorothy and Jessica love to talk about confidence and how to get it. They are co-founders of Confidence Builders International, a training and management development company that specializes in providing a happy environment for people who are learning the tough stuff they need to know to be great managers. The Confidence Builders training philosophy is pretty simple: *laughter precedes learning.*

Confidence Builders International serves many clients throughout the United States and is expanding into the international market. The flagship program is called *Focus Management*. It is designed to help managers learn every phase of the management process, from understanding corporate culture to the subject of this book, making excellent speeches and presentations.

Your Public Speaking Workout will show you the secrets of really good speakers. You can become a great speaker, too—And have fun doing it.

A Special Thanks to Charles E. Reilly, Jr.

In 1981, Charles E. Reilly, Jr. and I wrote a book, **The Power of In-Person Communications, Hammond Farrell, New York.** The book was fun to write and very well received. It's been on the bookshelves of lots of executives since the '80s. In the intervening years, I've taught presentation and public speaking skills to hundreds of individuals and many executive groups and it's been a joy to watch these people find out they can speak with ease.

Charles Reilly was my first mentor in this fascinating business of public speaking. He taught me how to recognize and bring out the hidden talents in every speaker. He taught me how to use humor in teaching, and I've used those lessons ever since.

Now it's time to write a new book for new readers. Many of the ideas we discussed in the first book are still here, bright and shiny as ever. I've added some new insights and some techniques I've worked with throughout the past twenty years or so. And Jessica Selasky, my daughter and co-author, has contributed her unique insights and business experience to broaden the scope of the book.

I want to thank Charles for showing me how to help people find the best of their best as public speakers. It's been a great trip so far.

Dorothy Lynn
December 2000

Acknowledgements

Thanks to Elizabeth Selasky, who is a true Confidence Builder. She encouraged her mom, Jessica, and her grandmother, Dorothy, to keep on going no matter what. Everyone knows you can't let a 14-year old down.

Thanks to Real Music, 85 Liberty Ship Way, Sausalito, CA 94965. Dorothy played the music from Kevin Kern's **In the Enchanted Garden** every time she sat down to write. This music is a writer's dream.

Thanks to the wonderful clients who tried our speaking techniques in the Confidence Builders seminars.

Thanks to friends and relatives who encouraged us every step of the way (including the 1/2 step).

To our terrific family who laughed with us along the way and who let us know they were always there for us: Chris, Tonya and Tyler Vikos; Robin Albritton, Rick Kaminski, and Morgan Kaminski; Jamie Blacksher and Elizabeth Selasky; and in memory of Aly Vikos, whose happy smile will remain embedded in our hearts forever. This is our gang.

Thanks to the great speakers who always inspire us.

Table of Contents

INTRODUCTION......................................1

STEP 1: ANALYZE YOUR FEAR OF PUBLIC SPEAKING......5

    1.1 Pounding Heart & Sweaty Palms 7

    1.2 Adrenaline in Action: 3 Ways to Control Fear 11

    1.3 A New Way to Look at Your Body Parts 15

STEP 2: NARROW YOUR FOCUS 17

    2.1 Pump Up Your Brain Power: Planning 19

    2.2 Combine Head and Heart: You & Your Audience 25

    2.3 Bare Bones & Skeletons: Speaking Extemporaneously ..33

    2.4 Brains at Work: Outlining and Ideamapping 34

STEP 3: ASSEMBLE THE PIECES AND PARTS OF YOUR SPEECH 45

    3.1 Let Your Fingers Do the Walking: Information Gathering 47

    3.2 Small Group Business Presentations 50

    3.3 Out of the Mouths: Strong Openings 52

    3.4 Shut Thy Mouth: Strong Closings 57

    3.5 Shaking the Skeleton: The Key Idea Outline 59

    3.6 Tickle Their Taste Buds: Anecdotes and Stories 64

    3.7 Belly Laughs and Silly Grins: Jokes & Humor 69

    3.8 Build that Muscle: The Body of the Speech 75

STEP 4: TACKLE THE DETAILS......................79

    4.1 Out of Body Experiences: Why Visual Aids? 81

    4.2 Off the Top of Your Head: Creating Titles 91

    4.3 Should I Memorize? (We Wish You Wouldn't) 93

    4.4 Using A Teleprompter 96

    4.5 Rough Drafting 97

    4.6 Sit On It: The Power of Editing 99

    4.7 Location, Location, Location... 103

STEP 5: OBSERVE YOURSELF 113

    5.1 Display Those Body Parts: Rehearse 115

    5.2 Be Natural, Be Prepared, Be Enthusiastic 116

    5.3 See Yourself Speaking: The Art of Visualization 122

    5.4 Step Up With PEP: Fabulous Introductions 124

    5.5 Sink Your Teeth Into This:
Eating Right For High Energy 127

STEP 6: MAKE A GREAT SPEECH 129

    6.1 Open Wide: Let the Speech Begin 131

    6.2 A Professional Approach 134

    6.3 Five Quick Ways To Calm Your Body 135

    6.4 Audiences Want The Best 136

    6.5 Put Your Mind At Ease 139

    6.6 Your Eyes: A Powerful Body Part 142

    6.7 Where Are Your Hands Anyway? 147

    6.8 Posture & Pacing 150

    6.9 Presence & Attitude 154

    6.10 At the Heart of the Matter:
Question & Answer Techniques 158

    6.11 The Checkup: Critiquing The Speech 164

THE HALF STEP: YOU 167

FREQUENTLY ASKED QUESTIONS 172

INDEX 179

Introduction

Many of the people we work with are successful in business or in other professions and yet, when it comes to speaking in public, they feel lost. This book will give readers the quick advice they need to feel totally comfortable every time they get up to speak. There's no need to worry about public speaking…we know this because we've seen so many people become terrific speakers after learning how to use their (you guessed it) body parts correctly.

We are the mother/daughter team of Dorothy Lynn and Jessica Selasky, and we are partners in a training business called Confidence Builders International. Our work is about helping people understand how confident they can be. We love to see people blossom as they learn the skills and techniques that will help them be better at what they do. The people who attend our training seminars are very special to us—they are the force behind all the work we do. And that's why we've decided to write this new book on speaking in public.

We were having what we call an Ideamapping or Brainstorming session one day, and we asked ourselves what people really want out of a book on public speaking. We played around with a lot of ideas, and in good brainstorming style, we didn't judge any of the words or ideas we came up with.

Suddenly, certain words flew out. One of the things we know for sure is that most people think there's some sort of big secret about getting up in front of people that very few speakers have figured out. Jessica said people really would love to be in on that secret. I said we talk a lot about body parts in our speeches—hands, eyes, mouths and so on. We wrote down lots of ideas. After about twenty minutes, we put these unrelated words together: *workouts, public speaking, and body parts* We came up with this idea—**Your Public Speaking Workout**: *Exercise Your Body Parts.*

How would we go about presenting these ideas? We'd use our unique 6 1/2 Step Method to help you build your speaking skills. Since using your various body parts and working them out for yourself are exactly the ideas we want to get across in this book, we had our title. We laughed a lot as we played with the captions for the body parts. You'll see examples of them throughout the book.

We enjoyed writing the book and it is our hope that you'll have fun reading it. AND...much more important, that you'll follow the 6 1/2 Step Method because the steps represent the heart of the book. There are solid tips to help you overcome any nervousness you might have about public speaking. There are sound techniques to help you develop your speech and good ideas about what to do when you're actually up there on the firing line with pounding heart, dry mouth, and wet hands...just some of the body parts you'll be learning about.

One method we use to help you make the material more valuable is through our **Work It Out** exercises. You'll find these exercises throughout the book. Whenever you see the **Work It Out** symbol, STOP and do the exercise.

Work It Out

We've found that to help people become expert at public speaking, practice is the key. You could attend ten seminars, read a hundred books, and watch a thousand speakers, and not one of these methods will do you a bit of good as a speaker **until the moment you stand up to speak.** We believe so strongly in this idea that the motto at Confidence Builders is *"What You Do Is What You Learn."* That means that you basically handle situations based on what you've learned about them so far. For example, if you've learned that riding a bike is easy, you'll never hesitate to jump on a bike, ride off and have a great time. If you've never tried it, or if you tried it once, fell down and skinned your knee, you'll probably avoid bike riding. If you've learned that people think you're shy, you may act shy for years and years and never understand why you always seem to feel uncomfortable around people. *What You Do Is What You Learn.* So let's begin to learn some new things about how to speak in public.

Standing up and trying out the techniques we'll share will make the difference for you, and that's why we've included **Work It Out** exercises. They'll get you up and moving toward your goal. Okay, it's not the same as being in front of a live audience, but we'll ask you to do that, too, as part of your practice sessions. You'll have fun and become an active participant in your own learning experience.

Why Do We Use the 6 1/2 Step Training Method?

At Confidence Builders, we use our unique 6 1/2 Step Training System for our programs, speeches, tapes, and books. The first six steps are designed to help you learn the material quickly and easily. Our test is always the same—can we identify the six essential elements someone needs to know in order to get started in a discipline such as speaking, writing, and listening? If we can identify the six most important elements, we know we're on the right track, and we can share that information with others. That's why we have the 6 1/2 Steps for you to follow. For this book we're focusing on all those body parts you use every time you speak—your **ANATOMY.**

>   Step One: **A**nalyze Your Fear of Public Speaking
>
>   Step Two: **N**arrow Your Focus
>
>   Step Three: **A**ssemble the Pieces and Parts of Your Speech
>
>   Step Four: **T**ackle the Details
>
>   Step Five: **O**bserve Yourself
>
>   Step Six: **M**ake a Great Speech
>
>   *Half Step:* **Y**OU: Enjoy the Speech

Whenever you get up to speak, your whole body participates in one way or another. It's how you use all those body parts that makes the difference. We'll talk about the importance of eye contact—we'll show you how to use your voice to say precisely what you want to say—how to use your hands so they're not flying around like wild geese—how to quit fidgeting and start connecting. It's amazing how important your body parts are when it comes to making a great speech.

That Extra Half Step

Let's address the extra half step of our 6 1/2 Step Training in more detail. The half step is the driving force behind the whole 6 1/2 Step Method. It's the fuel you need to get going with the new information you'll be learning as you go through the book.

How many times have you attended a seminar, read a book, or listened to a tape and left the experience excited about the information you'd received? And how many times have you been unsure of what to do next? How do you implement the new ideas? Our half step addresses that issue by asking you to go out and try the new ideas *immediately* to see if there is any improvement or change in your speaking ability. If you do, chances are better than good that you'll be happy with the results. So the half step requires *action* on your part. Take action! You'll be rewarded with a terrific speech.

The ideas in the book are based on over twenty years' experience giving speeches and working with people just like you—people who want to become powerful public speakers and to fully enjoy the experience. Thanks for spending time with us. We'll try to make your visit worthwhile.

Dorothy & Jessica, December 2000

Step 1

Analyze Your Fear of Public Speaking

*"A journey of
a thousand miles
must begin with
a single step."*

—Lao-Tzu

Step 1 Analyze Your Fear of Public Speaking

1.1 Pounding Heart & Sweaty Palms

If you've learned so far that public speaking is tough and scares most people, you've probably tended to avoid trying it. Makes sense. But maybe now you have no choice. Have you reached a point in your career where speaking in public is something you must do in order to remain successful? Or have you joined a community service organization that needs your help in getting the word out to people about your cause? Whatever your reason for picking up this book, you are going to go through a learning process—a shift in your thinking.

CEOs, sales professionals, doctors, teachers, product managers, aspiring actors, professional speakers, and even kids have tested the ideas presented here. The ideas work and they'll work for you.

Before we take a closer look at the all those body parts you use when you speak, we need to take your current speaking temperature.

Fear & Trembling Scale

| 1 | 2 | 3 | 4 | 5 | 6 | 7 | 8 | 9 | 10 |

Total Confidence   **Extreme Fear**

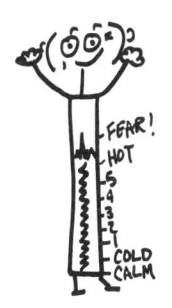

Check off the degree of fear you feel about public speaking, with 1 being the least and 10 being the greatest amount of fear you experience when you think about speaking. Would you like to change your number? What number represents your goal? Mark that number and then you'll clearly see the gap you need to fill in as we work through the pages of this book. For example, if you marked 6 and want to get to 4 on the Fear Scale, you have a minor gap and you just need to fine-tune your skills. But, if you marked 9 and you want to be at 3, your gap is a major one and you'll want to spend time getting to know the basics of good speaking as you work your way through the book.

When Fear Takes Over

Why are so many people afraid to speak in public? What is so frightening about standing up in front of an audience and sharing ideas? Some of you are starting to shake already, just at the thought of getting up to speak.

> *"Nothing in life is to be feared.*
> *It is only to be understood."*
> —Marie Curie

Fear is the dread of the unknown. Fear plays games with the mind. Once the mind is involved in a negative way, it can think of a million reasons to be scared. And as long as thoughts are allowed to go unchecked, FEAR remains. We've all known people who are afraid to fly. For those of us who are not afraid of those jumbo jets soaring through the sky, this fear seems out of proportion, especially since every study shows that flying in an airplane is safer by far than driving an automobile or walking across the street. It's not rational to fear flying. Tell that to the people who won't get into an airplane!

Fear of public speaking is real for the people who experience it. It's easy to fantasize about how stupid we'll feel when no words come out of our mouths and the audience is laughing at us, or when our ideas turn to jelly as we try to make sense of them up there, or when someone asks a question we cannot answer. Fantasy becomes reality in our minds and that's that.

When someone invites us to speak, we turn down the offer. And if we can't turn down the offer because it'll cost us a job or a promotion, we get up and speak and we hate every single minute, from the onset of the assignment until we sit down at the end of the speech, bitter and exhausted. It is almost assured that, with this mental conditioning, the speech will not work and many of our worst fantasies actually turn into realities. And so the fear continues and becomes worse and worse.

> *"Some terrible things happened in my lifetime—a few of which actually happened."*
> —Ben Franklin

How Can We Change?

What can we do right now to change this mind set? How can we begin to look forward to our speaking assignments? Tall order? For some of you, this is one of the tallest, for others, it's a matter of learning the tricks of the speaking trade and then you'll be fine with public speaking. No matter where you are on the FEAR SCALE, you can change. We've seen enough success stories to know that change is not only possible, but *probable* for people who are ready to learn how to speak in public. Yes, it will take time and effort, and only you know what you're willing to do to become a better speaker. If you think that just skimming through this book will do the trick, you're probably wrong. If you're willing to practice the skills we are going to share with you, you'll undoubtedly conquer any fear you have about speaking in public. It's up to you.

For now, why not take a moment to sit quietly and think about any fear you might have of public speaking. Is it holding you back from promotions or from getting the business you deserve? Is public speaking something you've been wanting to learn about for some time and just haven't gotten around to because of some hidden fear? Or, do you have a speech or presentation coming up in the next few days or weeks and are you feeling threatened by thoughts of making a fool of yourself? Whatever your reason, take this moment to know that fear of public speaking represents nothing more than a bad decision you made at some other time in your life. It is no longer reasonable for you to be afraid of public speaking. Help is at hand.

> *"Do the thing you are afraid to do and the death of fear is certain."*
> —Ralph Waldo Emerson

You Don't Need This Fear in Your Life

You can choose to eliminate the fear of public speaking forever. How would that make you feel? Imagine how it would be if every time someone asked you to make a speech, you could say with a smile, "I'd love to. How much time do I have?" If this is a goal of yours, settle on it. It can happen, and sooner than you think.

> *"You gain strength, courage and confidence by every experience in which you stop to look fear in the face."*
> —Eleanor Roosevelt

Work It Out

Take a moment or two to write down your thoughts about public speaking. Write a short paragraph describing any fears or concerns you have. Then finish the paragraph with a sentence or two about the goals you would like to achieve as a public speaker.

Self-Confidence

The first step is to develop the confidence of a speaker. How? If you can break each part down into manageable steps, your *unfounded* fears will begin to diminish and with practice, they'll eventually disappear altogether.

Notice we said *unfounded* fear...we know that the art of speaking in public, just like acting, requires some fear. That's the adrenaline push working for you to get you ready to perform and that's the positive fear that will give you the energy you need to do your best.

We're not advocating eliminating all fear and turning you into a talking robot that gets up and spits out words. Far from it. We want you to actually *enjoy* the experience. Unfounded fear prohibits this and it is that fear we want to help you get rid of forever. Let's quit talking about fear and do something about it.

1.2 Adrenaline in Action: 3 Ways to Control Fear

1. **Overprepare. This Simple Step Is One That Is Most Often Overlooked.**

   One of the questions we hear a lot in our Confidence Builders seminars is, *"What if they find out I don't know as much as I should about this subject? They're going to wonder why I'm the one up there talking."* Most people, it seems, have the idea that a speaker must be infallible when standing behind a lectern. This is an invalid thought. No one knows everything about a subject—even someone who is a world-renowned specialist will have some weak areas. This is expected and more important, accepted! Forget the idea that you must know every conceivable thing about your subject. What you can do to prevent nervousness is to <u>learn as much as you need to reach your own personal comfort level</u>. And you'll know when you've reached that point. The strange part is that you probably will not have to use the extra bit of information you've learned, but it sure helps your confidence level to know that, in fact, you do know a lot about your subject and the audience isn't going to look at you as if you're some kind of an impostor.

2. **Do your homework.**

   The second idea seems obvious, but for some people, doing the actual work involved in getting ready for a speech seems daunting. You must put the required time into it.

   ### A Startling Statistic

   This is probably a good time to share what we call a *startling statistic*. How long do you think it takes to prepare a 20-minute speech? In our seminars, people give answers anywhere from two hours to eight or ten hours. Their answers are all over the place. Experts in this field agree that it takes ***one hour*** of preparation time for ***every minute*** of a speech. Simple arithmetic tells us that it will take 20 hours to get ready for a 20-minute speech.

Formula
1 hour preparation time = 1 minute speech
20 hours preparation time = 20 minute speech

We usually don't use many exclamation points, but we think two are warranted here. 20 hours for 20 minutes!! That's an enormous commitment of time and energy. Most people are shocked when they learn this startling statistic. And most people have never devoted anything close to this amount of time in developing a speech. Of course, we don't mean that you sit down one fine day and spend the next twenty hours creating a speech and then go out and deliver it exhausted and shocked by the experience. That would probably be your one and only speech and no one would ever be able to get you up in front of an audience again.

You spread the hours over time. You'll spend a small percentage of your available time in planning, a larger chunk in the actual preparation of the words and visuals, and the most time fine-tuning and rehearsing.

An important piece of advice is not to be a deadliner—that's the person who procrastinates, hoping that the speech will somehow magically come together at the last minute. It won't. It's deadlining that gives public speaking a bad name. So, the first thing to realize is that you're going to have to bite the bullet and spend the time it takes to create and deliver a first-rate speech. The rewards of your effort will far exceed your investment of time.

3. **Be There & Be Present.**

   Before you walk onto the stage, tell yourself that you are going to be aware of everything that's happening while you speak. This means that you actually decide *to show up for your own speech*. Most speakers who admit to being afraid when they speak tell us that they somehow go through the motions, in a sense *pretending* to be up there speaking, but in their minds they are someplace else. Where are they? They put themselves on automatic pilot and say the words they've planned—usually as quickly as possible and then they say a quick *thank you* and hurry off the stage. When asked what they remember about the experience, the answer is *absolutely nothing*. That is not being present. If you are not present, the audience knows it and sits with hands folded politely, just waiting for you to finish and hoping your speech will not be too long. To be present means you can actually **see** individuals in the audience rather than defocusing and creating a big blur; it means that you pace yourself according to their needs; and it means that you literally look into their eyes all the time you're speaking. If you can do these things, you are really there in mind and spirit, and the audience knows it without a doubt and they go along with you, wherever you choose to take them.

> *"Do the thing and you will have the power."*
> —Ralph Waldo Emerson

Work It Out: Take Your Pulse

Here's an exercise we recommend to get you into the proper frame of mind every time you speak. We call it **Take Your Pulse.** This is a great way to get rid of any nervousness you might be experiencing prior to making a speech or presentation. This exercise will help you realize what a terrific person you are. It's a good idea, from time to time, to focus with laser beam accuracy on your strengths. Think about what you offer the world. What is it about you that makes you tick—strengths only please. It's much easier to list negatives, isn't it? We seem to keep an updated list of the things we don't do well, but for now, let's concentrate on your best qualities.

In the chart below, you'll see the numbers 1 through 10. Notice there is a line under the number 7. Make a list of 7 of your best qualities. Then stop. For example, are you *energetic*? Write it down. *Caring*? Write it down. Keep going until you have 7 one-word descriptions. Why do people like you?

TAKE YOUR PULSE

1.
2.
3.
4.
5.
6.
7. _____
8.
9.
10.

Who Are YOU?

Have you completed your list? How hard was it for you to come up with all 7? It's been interesting over the years of doing this exercise in our seminars to observe how people handle this assignment. Some dash off the list in seconds, but many people have a hard time writing down their positive attributes. They may struggle to get 3 and then start to look around the room to see how others are doing on this assignment. It's important to get to 7 because we need to call upon our own personal strengths every time we get up to speak. So, if you say you're *creative*, how will your creativity show up in your speech? Or if you say you are *enthusiastic*, are you using this quality every time you speak? Do your audiences see these characteristics in you?

What about numbers 8, 9, and 10? Ask someone else to give you his or her impressions of you. Write them down on your chart. It's important to identify your own strengths, but it can be equally important to learn what others have to say about you.

For example, suppose your boss adds the word *approachable* to your list. This would be an important insight for you because it means that people find it easy to talk with you. Or suppose a co-worker says you have a *sense of humor*. Wouldn't it be great to tap into that humor in your presentations and speeches?

Your list will provide valuable information because it bolsters your self-confidence and helps eliminate fear. We like to go over our lists before each presentation we make. It helps us realize we have a lot to offer an audience. That's better self-talk than saying things like "Oh, I'll be so nervous." "What if I forget where I am?" "Will I look foolish?" You know your own negative self talk. Choose not to focus on that. Check your positive pulse before each speech and you'll make better presentations.

1.3 A New Way to Look at Your Body Parts

Now that we've spent some time taking a look at how you see yourself, let's examine how others see you—see your body parts at work. Remember you use your body parts extensively every time you speak.

The speaking process starts with examining those body parts. You have to know how to have fun with the various parts of the body you use every time you speak in public. It's when speakers refuse to have fun that the idea of public speaking becomes frightening and dangerous to them. So let's begin by taking an inventory of the body parts you use every time you speak in public.

Every One of These Body Parts Comes into Play When You Speak in Public

1. Adrenal Glands
2. Brain
3. Diaphragm
4. Ears
5. Eyes
6. Eye Brows
7. Face
8. Feet
9. Fingers
10. Hands
11. Heart
12. Legs
13. Lips
14. Lungs
15. Mouth
16. Muscles
17. Nervous System
18. Shoulders
19. Soul
20. Stomach
21. Teeth
22. Vocal Chords

Others you can think of? _____

As you can see, the list of body parts is long, and we're going to be talking about most of them as we travel through the 6 1/2 Step Training System. Watch for them.

An Interesting Body Part: The Brain

One of the things we tell our students is that you become what you believe. In his book **Think & Grow Rich**, Napoleon Hill says, *"Whatever man can conceive and believe, he can achieve."* What does this mean? We think it means that you have complete control over what you think about any subject, and you can choose any scenario you like. Inside your brain is the key to your speaking success. You have so many ideas and thoughts to share about your subject that you could probably make ten speeches on a single topic and still have a hundred more ways to approach it. Our next step takes us into the most amazing body part, the **brain**. In STEP TWO we're going to begin to help you use your brain to *Narrow Your Focus* as we talk about how to start a speech or presentation from scratch.

> *"If we did all the things we are capable of doing, we would astound ourselves."*
> —Thomas Edison

Step 2

Narrow Your Focus

*"Part of success
is preparation
on purpose."*

—Jim Rohn

Step 2 Narrow Your Focus

2.1 Pump Up Your Brain Power: Planning

The brain has billions of cells and an infallible memory. It is the storehouse of your life's experiences. Your brain contains the inventory you're going to need every time you speak in public. This 3-pound miracle is filled with both brilliant and stupid ideas, imaginative and ordinary solutions. This body part is the one you depend on most when it comes to creating a speech. It's the life force that makes you the unique person you are. That's because each of us uses our brainpower in different ways. You can decide to use it to make a mediocre presentation or a spectacular speech that results in a standing ovation. It's always your choice.

You take yourself with you wherever you go. Your thoughts actually create your reality, so if you think that public speaking makes you scared, you'll be scared. And if you think you can make a great speech, you can.

Obviously you want to learn new concepts about speaking and you want to apply these new ideas. This will create a new way of thinking for you. Won't it be wonderful to consider public speaking a joy, an exciting and challenging part of your life?

> *"To be a good speaker in public, you must be a good thinker in private."*
> —Anon

Planning: Brainpower in Action

How do you know where to begin when you have to make a speech? There are so many ideas floating around in your head, how do you capture just the right ones? As Jessica's daughter, Elizabeth says,

"I can't clean my room because I just don't know where to start." The task seems overwhelming. But once she gets started, her room is cleaned in no time.

Start by using one of your most important body parts, your brain. You're going to have to come up with a simple way to get started every time you have to make a speech. We simply refer to it as PLANNING. The word planning sounds pretty formal, doesn't it? Planning is simply recognizing where you are now, where you'd like to go, and how you're going to get there.

Planning To Develop A Speech

1. **Choose the results you want to achieve: Purpose or *so that* Formula**
2. **Know something about your topic and your audience: T-Bar Analysis**
3. **Select the best way to develop ideas from point A to point Z: Ideamapping**

We're going to go step-by-step through the process, teaching you along the way how to make the time you spend on speaking pay off. You're getting ready to deliver the best speech you've ever made. You and your audience are going to enjoy every minute of that speech.

Choose the Result You Want to Achieve: Purpose

The Brain at Work

The first step in the planning process is to decide just what it is you're going to be talking about. The easiest way is to begin by writing a *general-purpose statement* for the speech in a short sentence or phrase. Try to capture your overall intention for the speech. Remember that this is just to get you started on the process. Don't worry too much at this point about making this sentence or phrase perfect. We call it a *first thought* idea.

We've found that the first thoughts we have about a subject tend to be too obvious, superficial, and are often nothing more than clichés. It seems that the brain has to go through a series of ideas, starting with the simple to reach the more complex. If we choose to accept our first thoughts, we'll usually wind up with ordinary, everyday thoughts that are just not very interesting. And that is not our goal, is it?

The Amazing *so that* Formula

We recommend a system that helps speakers narrow their focus and helps them decide, rather quickly, the true purpose of the speech. It's called the *so that* formula. We've worked with this idea for several years now and the results are nothing short of remarkable.

These two simple words can help you find the heart of your speech before you spend a lot of unnecessary time trying on one idea after another and still coming up short most of the time.

The *so that* formula forces you to think. Here's how it works: You start with that general-purpose statement (first thought)—a sentence, phrase or word will do. Write it down and think about it for a couple of seconds.

Example of a First Thought Idea

General Purpose Statement: *I want to speak to senior management about introducing employee development and training programs throughout the organization.*

This general purpose statement is fine as far as it goes, but it's too broad, isn't it? If you stop right there and begin to develop the speech based on your first idea, you're probably going to miss your real reason for giving the speech. Where can you go with a broad topic such as **Employee Development & Training**? You must begin to narrow your focus so the ideas become more manageable.

Let's insert the *so that* Formula and see what happens:

so that #1

I want to talk about introducing employee development and training programs *so that* senior management understands that well-trained employees are more productive and that leads to bottom line results.

Okay, that's a good start.

Delve deeper:

so that #2:

I want senior managers to recognize how important training is *so that* they will agree that employee development should be a key consideration for our company's long-term future success and will support the effort.

Now you're beginning to focus on a real issue you can address in your presentation.

Go deeper:

so that #3:

Training is one of the key ingredients to success *so that* our people will become the best in the field and that will make our organization better and more competitive.

Aha! Now you've got something to work with. Your specific purpose statement now might look something like this:

I will speak to senior management about how proper and effective training and employee development will help to guarantee us the competitive edge we need in our industry. Training is a worthwhile investment.

Would you agree that you could develop a really good speech based on this more narrow focus? The point here is that if you had developed the speech based on your more superficial first thought, it would be a DIFFERENT speech, and, in most cases, it would not be as effective as the one that comes out of using the simple *so that* formula.

One idea to note: Using the *so that* Formula will lead everyone who uses it to reach different conclusions, so if you're starting with the general idea concerning employee development or training, your *so that* will probably lead in entirely different directions from the example we've given here. There's no one right way to create a speech; the *so that* formula simply helps you focus more clearly on what you really want and need to say.

We've had great success teaching the formula. Many of our clients have reported that they love to use it because it helps them think more clearly. And here's the result: their speeches and presentations work better for them.

Work It Out

Would you like to try the ***so that*** formula? We think you'll find it will become one of the most valuable tools in your public speaking tool kit.

To begin, let's practice on a general topic to see how the process works. We'll start with a general-purpose statement and then apply the ***so that*** formula.

Example:

General Purpose: I want to announce our annual company picnic at the company meeting.

Your first ***so that:*** I want to tell people about the picnic so that they will know we're having one and where it is, etc.

Your second ***so that:*** I want people to know that the company picnic will be a lot of fun so that it will be worth their time and attention.

Your third ***so that:*** I want to let people know that this will be the best picnic we've ever had, with all sorts of games and food and a great day so that they will know we really appreciate the hard work everyone has done and this is our chance to just have a terrific time getting to know our co-workers better.

Your final Purpose Statement: This presentation will be to let our people know how much we appreciate them. We're happy to invite them to relax and enjoy a wonderful day of fun, food, and entertainment.

Can you see how the thoughts developed as we kept asking our ***so that*** questions? This presentation will be livelier and more directed because we dug deeper.

Now it's your turn to try one:

General Purpose: **I want to talk about the high rate of turnover in my company.**

First *so that:*_____

Second *so that:* _____

Third *so that:*_____

Your Final Purpose Statement: _____

How did you do? Talking about high turnover rates is important, but what was the real purpose of this presentation? We usually need two or three sets of the *so that* formula to reach the stage that says, "Aha this is it." It could take more (or less) depending upon the quality of your first thought.

Why not try to use the formula for one of your own speeches? Start with the general purpose and then keep going until you know you've narrowed down your focus.

General Purpose Statement: _____

First *so that:*_____

Second *so that:* _____

Third *so that:*_____

Your Final Purpose Statement: _____

Did the formula work for you? In terms of the *one hour per minute* statistic we talked about earlier, this process usually takes about ten minutes, so although it's a critical step, it doesn't take too much of your overall allotted time.

It's important to realize at this point that the final purpose statement actually drives the whole speech. If you come up with one purpose, the speech will go one way. If you come up with another, the focus will shift. With *no controlled purpose statement* you'll have a hodgepodge of ideas that usually end up confusing the audience, and that's not what you want.

2.2 Combine Head and Heart: You & Your Audience

Now that you have the purpose of the speech clearly in mind, it's time to move on to the next phase of the plan—to choose the actual topics you want to cover based on the final purpose statement.

Your Greatest Fear!

We know from years of speech coaching experience that the greatest fear you have about public speaking is that someone in the audience will think you don't know what you're talking about. We mentioned this number one fear in Step One. **You're afraid you'll look like a fool.** If you stop and analyze this fear for a minute, you'll see that the chances of this happening are remote.

The fact of the matter is the complete opposite of your fear—**you actually know too much**. Let's face it, you're not going to be asked to speak on a subject that is totally foreign to you. No one is going to ask you to make a speech about nuclear physics if you're a buyer for a department store. You actually know volumes about your subject. Most people have so many ideas about the subject they'll be speaking about, they find it hard to sort all of the ideas out.

If Everything is Important, Nothing is Important

Your *real* task is to figure out what information you can expect the audience to grasp in the amount of time you have available. You cannot tell the audience everything you know. Think about this: *If everything is important, nothing is important.*

What this means is that you must choose the few critical points you want to share on your subject. It's your responsibility to weed out the interesting but nonessential details. **This is one of the toughest jobs most speakers face.** You have to focus with laser-like precision on the key elements you want to share and discard the rest.

Perhaps you'll be able to discuss some of the juicier items later when you enter the Q & A portion of the speech. (We have some great tips for handling these sessions in Step Six: Make A Great Speech). Keep in mind that your audience deserves to hear the results of your best thinking. Let's move on to the next phase of your planning process. We call it the **T-Bar Analysis.**

T-Bar Analysis

To capture your best thinking, we recommend using a T-Bar Analysis as the next logical step in planning the speech because it forces you to choose the items you plan to address, and it helps you figure out what your audience wants and needs to know.

T-Bar

I must say:	**My audience needs & wants to know:**
1.	
2.	
3.	

Here's how to use the T-Bar. On the left side, under the words *I must say*, write down the three ideas you absolutely must get across if your speech is to be successful. We like to limit the number of choices to *three* for the following reasons:

1. Most people can understand material presented in sequences of 3 main ideas at a time. Our studies have shown that if you try to make 7, 8 or 10 points, there is a good chance that none of them will stand out.

2. It's easier for you to work on the actual preparation of your speech when you focus on 3 key points rather than allowing yourself to ramble on and on about ideas that might be interesting, but not important. *To ramble is a cardinal sin for a good speaker.* (And you're going to be a great speaker by the time you finish this course in a book.)

3. Selecting your three main points at this stage of the planning process enables you to concentrate on researching and gathering the precise information you'll need, which will save time in the long run and help you stay focused.

These points come from the final purpose statement, which is based on the results of the ***so that*** formula. See how it all begins to tie together in a nice neat little package?

Sub-Points

Once you've selected the three key ideas, you'll want to prioritize them into order of 1-2-3, with the most important thing you want to discuss first and so on. There will be several sub-points you'll develop out of each of the main points. That will come later. In the early stages of the planning process, you're trying to establish the focus of the speech. The details will flow easily out of this step.

You'll be happy to know that this part of the planning process takes very little time. You can usually come up with your 3 main points in ten minutes or less. Think of the time it will save as you flesh out the speech itself. So a small time commitment at this point has a tremendous payoff later on.

What About the Right Side of the T-Bar? Who's Who In the Audience?

On the right hand side of the T-Bar, we concentrate on what the audience wants and needs to know. Why is this important? Most careful speakers are pretty good at working out the information on the left side. They want to be sure to get their main points across and that's great as far as it goes.

Truly great speakers go to another level of thinking. They move over to the right hand side of the T-Bar and begin to analyze their audience. This one action alone will create a huge difference in the way you develop your presentation. Once you have a feeling for what the audience wants and needs, you can begin to address these issues. Better to guess wrong than not to think about the audience at all.

Here's how to go about this part of the planning process. Take a couple of minutes to think about who's who in your audience. This is an exercise in *probability thinking*. You can never get totally into the minds of others, but you can predict certain behaviors when you take the time to think about it.

So, in this case, what you want to think about first is how many people will be in the audience. What are their concerns? Our experience tells us their first concern is their own creature comfort. The more comfortable people are, the more likely they are to listen to a speaker. Although as a speaker you might not have total control of the seating arrangements or room conditions, it's wise to think about the impact of uncomfortable chairs, obstructed views, room temperature, and so on. (More about optimal seating plans in Step Four: Tackle the Details.)

Some Quick Tips

For example, if you know that the room you'll be speaking in will be hard on the audience, you'll want to consider that fact as you plan your remarks. Consider the following ideas:

1. Plan frequent stretch breaks
2. Use humor to ease tensions
3. Provide water
4. Provide non-sticky mints
5. Plan extra refreshment breaks

Sound odd? Off the subject? Not really. Part of the success every good speaker enjoys comes from paying attention to details. Many speakers simply overlook the basics and pay a stiff price. Often they don't even know why their speech failed. It could be as basic as a room that's too cold or a seat that's too hard.

Ask yourself who will be in your audience. Can you create a profile of the type of person who will attend? If your presentation is to a potential customer, what do you know about him or her? Is he the type of person who wants the facts and only the facts? Or is she a person who wants to have lots of information to ponder before making a decision? These are critical factors to consider as you plan your presentation. Write your observations down on the right side of the T-Bar. For example, is Sam demanding? Leslie impatient? Linda detail oriented? Does Terry have a great sense of humor? The more details you know about the individual members of your audience, the better your chances are of reaching them.

Suppose you're giving a presentation at your company's convention. Who will be in the audience? Will the CEO be there? Will the board of directors attend? What do they want to hear and see? Do you know that as a rule they like to get right to the point or do you know they like to be entertained first and then get down to business? Obviously, each case is different and unique. The time you spend filling out the right side of the T-Bar will pay off handsomely when you get up to speak.

The audience *needs* to know the ideas you are going to present based on the left side of your T-Bar analysis. This is the heart of your presentation. But what the audience *wants* to know can be quite different. For example, you might need to tell an audience that there will be significant cutbacks and downsizing due to poor results. They need to know this information, right? But what do they *want* to know? This is their immediate question, "What's going to happen to me?"

So often, speakers make a mistake in underestimating the amount of time most audiences listen *subjectively* rather than *objectively*. In the example about downsizing, as soon as you start talking about bad news, most people will focus on what that information means to them personally, and you can bet they'll miss the next five minutes of the speech. Even if you have some great solutions to offer, your ideas could be lost if a large segment of the audience has tuned out.

What can you do to avoid this common pitfall? In your planning process, write this probability: *people will be upset*. Put this idea on the right side of the T-Bar. Then think about what you must say to hold audience interest rather than lose it, or worse, alienate the very people you want to inform.

In the example about downsizing, a simple statement such as *"I know how upsetting this news is, so I've prepared a handout for you that shows exactly what is going to happen in each department."*

You could pass out the handout and give the audience a few minutes to absorb the information before going on to the next point. Or, you might want to simply stop the presentation and put people into small groups for a couple of minutes to talk about the upsetting news. In either case, you've allowed the audience to process the information *before* going on with the facts you need to deliver. If you don't plan for this, you stand a good chance of losing your audience. And you never want that to happen.

How Can I Use the T-Bar to Analyze People I Know?

Another way to use the right side of the T-Bar is to focus on an individual's traits or common responses—expected behaviors in different situations. For example, if you're speaking to a group of your peers, people you know very well, it would be beneficial to spend a few minutes thinking about each person in terms of what you think his or her personality traits are.

Suppose Mark is known as a hard driving, results oriented manager. As you plan your presentation, you'll want to try to understand his needs as a listener. He will not be interested in the finer details of your presentation. He wants to know the facts and what these facts will mean to him. What would you want to include in your speech if you had someone like Mark in your audience? Know that Mark will probably skip the niceties, but he'll get the point.

But what if Sandy is a relationship-oriented type of manager? She'll be mostly interested in hearing how the information you're giving can be used to handle people. She'll pay particular attention to the parts that relate to the human side of the enterprise.

And how about a third type? Melissa is interested in getting all the details before she'll buy into a project or accept a change. Once she hears how to go about doing something, she'll be the one who will make sure it happens. Add something in your speech about the details of the project. So now you have at least three different types and there are more. Part of your job as a speaker is to figure out, in advance, how to reach everyone in the audience. You're going to have to hit some of each person's "hot" buttons if your presentation is going to be a success.

This is not as difficult as it sounds. We recommend spending a fair amount of time on the audience analysis, because the payoff is tremendous. The people in the audience will respond more favorably to your remarks because they'll see themselves in the picture you paint. Remember, however, that this part of your plan is not precise, it's still a guessing game at this point—an educated guess, yet far better than no guess at all.

How About People I Don't Know?

You may be wondering how you can do this T-Bar analysis for a public audience, for people you don't know. You can still do the analysis based on some inferences you can draw based on the subject you're addressing. Who would be interested in hearing this speech? Why? What are some common characteristics you can identify?

For example, suppose you are in the financial investments business and your company offers financial advice seminars. The seminars are advertised in the local press or maybe on the radio. The public is invited to attend. What do you know about most people who would attend this kind of seminar? They are undoubtedly interested in making better investments. Some of them might be getting ready to retire and they need to learn what to do about pension funds. Others might be young professionals just getting started with an investment program.

What is the one common thread for all of these people? They all want to know how to make their money work for them and everyone is worried about making wrong financial decisions. Investing money creates tension for most people. As the speaker, you know you must say something during the presentation to make the audience relax and understand that you represent a good, solid reputable company and they have nothing to fear—they can trust you. Your T-Bar analysis will help you reach this decision, and then it's up to you to figure out what to say to develop audience confidence.

We do a lot of work with insurance companies. When we help participants in our seminars develop the right side of the T-Bar, we talk about the common characteristics found in people who own insurance policies. We know they want to feel safe and they want to feel that they can depend on the company to be there when they need them. The Allstate motto is a great example of understanding what a policyholder wants. "You're in Good Hands with Allstate." The feeling you get when you hear that is that you're safe. And the theme of State Farm: "Like a good neighbor, State Farm is there," tells its customers that State Farm is just like someone they know and can depend upon. At Teachers' Insurance, where we've done training seminars for more than ten years now, their motto is "Insuring the Future for Those Who Shape It." That's a nice tribute to the teachers of this country and it gives the teachers a sense of trust in the company that handles and invests their hard-earned money.

These themes capture the essence of the idea we're talking about—safety and trust. A good speaker will take the time to understand how an audience *feels* as much as how it *thinks*. When you reach an audience's heart, you've created a bond, and that's what good speakers do. The ***so that*** formula and **T-Bar Analysis** are great tools to help you know before you begin writing any words, how to focus on the real issues you want to address in your speech.

Work It Out

Why don't you take some time to do your own T-Bar Analysis to find out for yourself just how it works. If you are currently working on a speech, go through the whole process from the general purpose and ***so that*** formula through both the left and right sides of the T-Bar.

Use the ***so that*** Formula:

General purpose:

So that…
So that…
So that…

The final purpose statement:

Do the T-Bar Analysis:

I must say:	My audience needs & wants:

2.3 Bare Bones & Skeletons: Speaking Extemporaneously

Understand the Difference Between Ad Libbing and Extemporaneous Speaking

So far you have a little T-Bar chart. Just like the little old lady who asked, "Where's the beef?" you may be asking, "Where's the speech?" Soon. Like so many things in life, public speaking is a process, with one idea building upon another. A speech doesn't suddenly pop into your mind and out of your mouth. We're sure there have been occasions when people have given so called ad lib speeches that have been brilliant, but these instances are rare.

Select the Best Way to Develop Ideas

When you ad lib, you are speaking directly from thought to word with no stops in-between to consider the consequences of what you're saying. The thoughts that pop into your head pour out of your mouth with little or no editing. The words *ad lib* come from the Latin *ad libitum*, which means at *one's pleasure*. Ad libbing can be a lot of fun, especially when a person has a wonderful, rich sense of humor. You probably have some friends who are good at it. It's an art form. Charles Reilly, Dorothy's speech mentor, was a great ad libber. The brilliant actor, Robin Williams, takes the idea of ad libbing to a whole new dimension. If you've ever seen him interviewed on a talk show, you know what we mean. Ideas materialize and fall out of his mouth at an alarming rate of speed.

On the other hand, your goal is to speak extemporaneously. Here is the dictionary definition of the word **extemporaneous:** *previously planned but delivered with the help of few or no notes.* This is precisely what you want to do as a public speaker.

You want to be able to get up in front of any audience and speak to them, look at them, be with them. You cannot do all these things if you have too many slides and you concentrate on the slides more than on the audience. You cannot be present for them if you are glued to a manuscript or if your notes are so copious that you must refer to them so often the speech sounds mechanically reproduced.

Ad lib once in a while, and refer to your notes every so often, but speak *extemporaneously* if you want to discover the great speaker inside you.

2.4 Brains at Work: Outlining and Ideamapping

How do you organize your thoughts so you can speak extemporaneously? Some experts recommend outlining. Do you remember the Roman Numeral outlines we used in school? They looked like this:

Roman Numeral Outlining:

I. **Major Theme One**
    A.
    B.
    C.
        a.
        b.
        c.
            1.
            2.
            3.

II. **Major Theme Two**
    A.
    B.
        a.
        b.

(And don't forget—you can't have an A without a B or a 1 without a 2.)

We know how well this method works for a lot of people. If this is your preferred method, by all means use it. However, know outlining doesn't always work well for people with a more "right brained" mentality.

Narrow Your Focus

Dorothy's Story:

I have a confession to make. I was an English Major in college. Of course, we were asked to write hundreds of papers and essays and to submit our outlines to show how our thoughts developed. I never, not ever, completed the outline until after I had written the entire paper. I could fill in the blanks on the major topics, but I had a hard time filling in all those sub, sub topics. That requires linear thinking and my mind just does not work that way. Now, there are many people reading this book who have no trouble whatsoever with outlining and I applaud you. We are fortunate to have you in this world. However, are there any readers out there who outlined after the fact as I did? I'll bet I know the answer to that question.

Later, we're going to show you how to develop the ideas for your speech or presentation using what we call a Key Idea Outline, but first we want to share some exciting insights about the way human beings process information. After all, preparing a speech is about going through the process of selecting and categorizing information, isn't it? The thinking method we're going to share will help you gather the many and diverse thoughts you'll need to create a memorable speech. It's the step we recommend trying just before you create the Key Idea Outline.

Brains at Work

IDEAMAPPING: Using the Right/Left Brain Theory

"Once the human brain realizes that it can associate anything with anything else, it will almost instantaneously find associations, especially when given the trigger of an additional stimulus."

—Tony Buzan, **The Mind Map Book**, 1996

A few years ago at Confidence Builders, we learned about a method for processing information that hit home and makes absolute sense. This method relies on the left brain/right brain model of thinking.

Prior to the late 1960s, scientists were not clear about the precise way the brain processes information. New information became available that shows that the cortex of the brain is separated into two halves, divided by a thick band of nerves called the Corpus Callosum, which transmits ideas back and forth. The left side of the cerebral cortex is responsible for processing our logical, analytical thoughts. On the left side, we deal with words, numbers, and all sorts of linear thinking.

Think about school. In school we're taught to use this left side, and we rely on it to do math, to read, to write, to memorize and to solve problems—vital information for living in this society.

On the right side, there is another whole, complementary set of processes. Here we deal with imagination, color, art, rhythm, creativity, and music. We see the whole picture at once. We appreciate a sunset or a wonderful piece of music just because these marvels are there, not to analyze, but to simply enjoy. Certain experiences enrich our lives with beauty and serenity. Think of how you feel when you listen to music that really touches you. You become one with the sounds and the fantasies the music creates. All of this happens primarily on the right side of your brain.

To be fully alive, we need to tap into both sides of the brain. Think of Leonardo da Vinci. He was one of the most superb artists the world has ever seen (right brain) and a brilliant inventor (left brain).

Or how about Albert Einstein? It is reported that he used to wander around the streets of Princeton, New Jersey, lost in a reverie of some kind (right brain), until he had a flash of insight. Then he would rush back to his home and write a formula (left brain). You have this same ability. Don't you sometimes daydream about an idea, and then suddenly, seemingly out of nowhere, the perfect idea crystallizes? That's integrating right and left brain functions.

Left or Right?

How about this example? You lose a valuable ring. You logically review where you were the last time you wore it. (left brain) You look in the jewelry box, where you usually keep it, you check the top of the night stand and the bathroom sink. Nothing. You begin to look in unusual places—behind the bed, under a stack of newspapers. Still nothing. You've exhausted the logical sequences. (left brain)

You decide to visualize. You can actually see yourself wearing the ring. (right brain) You know you had it when you returned from Cousin Anne's wedding reception.

Where is that ring? You decide to sit quietly for a few minutes and just calm down. You sit still for a while and suddenly you get up, walk right over to the nightstand and there's the ring in the drawer (right brain). You now remember that you put it there because you forgot to take it off and put it in the jewelry box before you went to bed so you just dropped it into the drawer of the night stand for safe keeping. Now you recall with total clarity that you had decided that it would be fine to drop the ring into the drawer. (left brain) So, finding your ring became an integrated effort between your left and right brain—a marriage of logic and imagination.

Can We Create Synergy?

We can use a similar sequence of thought to capture ideas about a speech we are preparing. If we decide to use traditional outlining methods (for example using the Roman Numeral method described earlier), we're using left brain thinking pretty exclusively. That's perfectly all right, but research has shown that we can make our thoughts come much faster if we tap into the right side of the brain first and then go back to the logic of the left. That is, we want to shut down the logical left for a little while to find out what impressions and knowledge are sitting on the right side.

As you can imagine, it's very difficult to shut down the left side of our brains. We are logical human beings, after all, and we could not survive without the order the left brain represents. However, the logical left can be very limiting. It's the imaginative right that can see things in new, different, and sometimes better ways. The right side can create a whole new idea for the left side to work on. It's a wonderful synergy we're looking for.

Ideamapping for Creating Speeches

We're going to describe how to tap into the right side of your brain. This is fun and easy. Most people love to learn how to use this relatively new tool.

> To begin, get a piece of plain white paper ready. Turn it on the horizontal like this.
>
> And, if you have some easily accessible, get some colored pencils or crayons.
>
> We'll be using them in a few minutes.

We want to turn this paper on its side for two reasons. First, we want to get away from the traditional left-brained view of a piece of paper as something to take notes on because it's vertical and we start writing from the top left and go logically from word to word, sentence to sentence, paragraph to paragraph. That's pretty left-brained isn't it? We want to break through this barrier for this exercise. The other reason for turning the paper on its side is that we want to create a drawing rather than a linear set of words written from left to right on a vertical sheet of paper.

We call this technique Ideamapping, others call it Mindmapping™, Webbing, Clustering, and Spidering. The basic idea is the same for all of these methods—it's an opportunity to shut down the left side of the brain and tap into the right side *on purpose.*

Tony Buzan & Mindmapping

British author and lecturer, Tony Buzan, was the first person to popularize the notion of tapping into the right side of the brain on purpose. He created the popular system he calls Mindmapping™ (and we call Ideamapping).

The medical community had studied the brain and had written about discoveries in the medical journals, but it was Tony Buzan who recognized the importance of teaching average people how to use the vast resources available through accessing the right brain. In his book, **Use Both Sides of Your Brain**, he offers a systematic approach that teaches the reader exactly how to use the vast amount of information contained in the right brain.

We call our approach *Ideamapping* because we're interested in helping potential speakers find the ideas they need for their speeches, and we want them to be able to find them quickly and easily. *Ideamapping* is a wonderful way to discover what you already know about a subject. This method helps you tap into information that otherwise might be hidden to you because it's coming from your creative side rather than your logical side. That's the power behind this technique.

Be a Kid Again

What we are trying to do with Ideamapping is to recapture some of the right-brained innocence and intelligence of a child. Since a child's experience and knowledge is limited, it relies primarily on the right brain to function. You'll see young kids playing house or Laser Tag—games that are highly imaginative. They are using basically right-brained strategies.

Work It Out

Think back to when you were in first grade. Can you remember your eager little self? Your teacher asks you to draw a picture of your house and without hesitation, you begin to draw.

Do it now! Take that paper you've placed on the horizontal, stop reading, and draw a picture of your house as if you were a six-year old kid in first grade. Go ahead. Take three minutes to do this. It'll be fun. Use your favorite colored pencils.

Was it fun? How does your house look?

As a first grader, you didn't say to the teacher, "Excuse me. I need a drafting table and a slide rule." No. You just drew and the drawing represented your house or apartment and it was beautiful. The teacher told you it was beautiful. What happened when you got home and showed the picture of your house to your mother? Right onto the refrigerator door for all to see and admire. Your mother was proud of your work—and you felt good!

Little by little most of us learn to hold back the right brain imagination as we lean more and more toward the logical left brain side. That's a normal part of the educational process. Today we'd feel a little foolish if someone asked us to draw a picture of our house because now we know more about construction and balance, etc. Your imagination remains though, and Ideamapping will help you extract your ideas better and faster. That's why we recommend it, because it helps our clients find the answers to their questions quickly and efficiently.

Some Things to Consider as You Begin to Ideamap

Get another piece of unlined paper and place it on the horizontal. Tony Buzan recommends using colored pencils because *color excites the imagination.* If you have colored pencils, markers or crayons available, by all means use them, but if you don't, go ahead anyway—the result will still be outstanding.

It's the freedom of uncensored, random thought you're looking for. This exercise should last approximately three minutes because after that period of time, the left brain starts to rebel and wants to get back into the act.

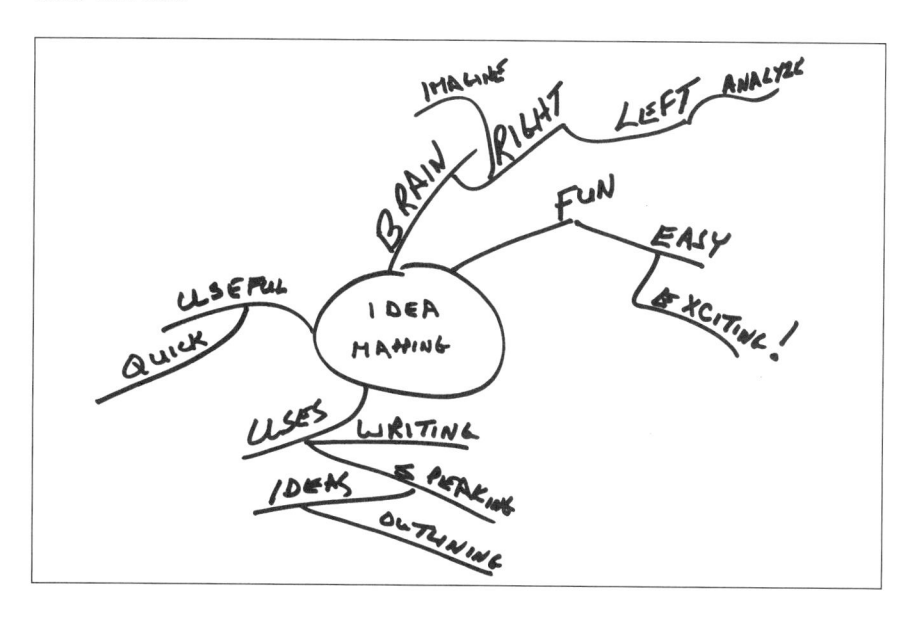

Work It Out
Here's How to Begin:

Go to the center of the paper and write a key word or short phrase and put a circle around it. This will become the focal point of your Ideamap. For this exercise, you might want to use the Final Purpose statement you came up with as you practiced using the ***so that*** Formula. Distill the thought into a single word or a short phrase or even a picture that captures your theme.

Set your timer or watch for three minutes. Next, look at the word, words or picture in the circle for a few seconds and let your mind wander around them. Then begin to jot down, quickly and without evaluation, every thought that enters your mind, one word at a time and one line to a word. It is recommended that you print the words so they are easy to write and to read later.

Leap from one idea to another until you run out of ideas. Do not think too hard (that would indicate your left brain is at work rather than your right.)

Each word you think of will trigger another. Write every one down and do not decide which are good words and which are not. Write every word because sometimes a word that seems out of context will link with another that will help crystallize your thinking on a subject. Keep writing as fast as your thoughts appear. Do not stop to reflect. Keep going.

When you finally reach a point where you seem to have run out of connections, go back to the center circle, look at the trigger words there, and begin to create another spoke about another facet of the Purpose statement. If you're using colored pencils, change colors. This will help your right brain work even better. Repeat the cycle, coming back to the center each time you need fresh ideas.

When your three minutes are up, take a look at what you have. You'll be amazed at the ideas you've been able to generate in this short period of time. Sometimes you'll remember an anecdote you can use in the speech, or you'll remember a startling statistic you can use to drive home a point in the speech. Often, you'll come up with a whole new idea you hadn't even considered before. That's one of the best uses of Ideamapping. The magical thinking that's going on in the right brain might help you come up with the perfect answer to a thorny problem you've been grappling with.

At first glance your Ideamap may look like a bunch of random words strewn across a page, but there is important information hidden inside those scribbles.

The next step is to take the ideas you've written and bring left-brained logic into play. As you look at the Ideamap, you'll begin to see new ideas and patterns of thought beginning to take shape. Now you'll be able to arrange these ideas in logical order, so you actually wind up with a usable outline.

This is a much faster, and in our opinion a much more enjoyable, way to create an outline than the old Roman Numeral method. Your right brain quickly pops out a variety of ideas you can use for your speech. Of course, you will not be able to use every idea you get during Ideamapping because you get so many. Your left brain will step in and sort out what you need for the speech or presentation. This is the left-brained activity that makes sense out of your right-brained 'scribbles.' Creating an Ideamap is an exciting and profitable use of your time.

Ideamap example 2

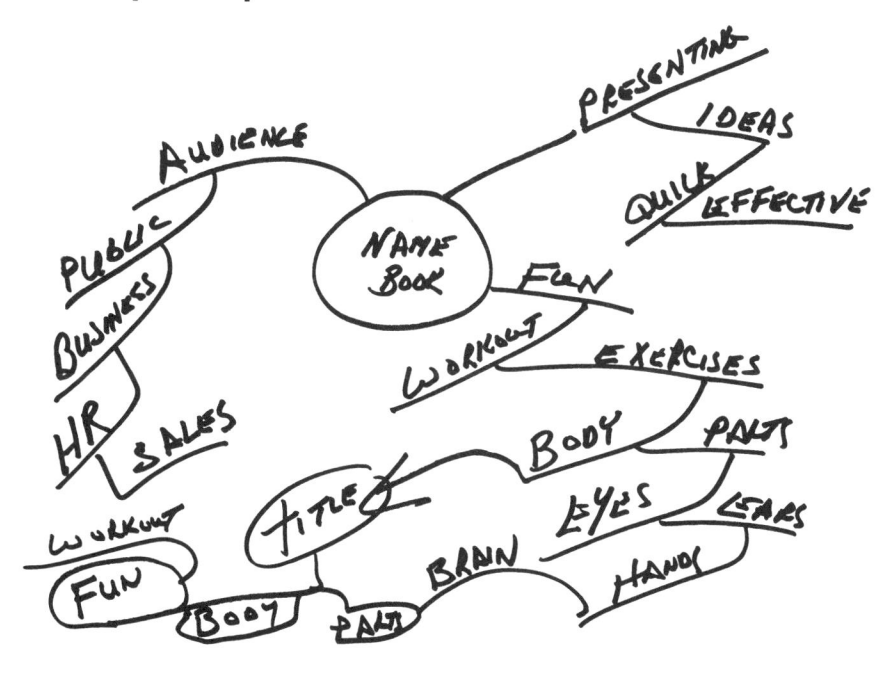

Go For It!

How do you like this organizing tool? While it is not for everyone, this new way of thinking has made a tremendous difference, not only in the quantity of ideas students in our seminars are able to generate, but also the *quality* of these ideas.

Sometimes we're shocked to find out how much people actually know about a subject. The facts and impressions are often hidden deep within the brain, but they are there nonetheless. In Richard Restek's book, **The Brain,** he says, "...the human brain can store more information than all the libraries in the world." That's one of those startling observations, isn't it? It helps us to stop and think about the magnificence of our brains.

Some psychologists tell us that we don't use much of our brain power. Back in the sixties and seventies they used to say we used approximately ten percent of our brains. Today, in the 21st Century, these psychologists are saying most of us use *less than one percent* of our brainpower. Don't get discouraged by that statistic. Think of all we've been able to do with this one percent: get a man on the moon, build magnificent skyscrapers, investigate Mars, search for a cure for cancer, design startling computers, and so on. Imagine what the future holds if we can release more of our brainpower.

Public speaking provides you with a wonderful opportunity to share what you know with others. The steps we've discussed so far will help you tap into your many and varied sources of information. As you go along in the organization process, a picture begins to form of not only what you are going to say, but how you're going to say it.

Once you've completed your Roman Numeral Outlining or *Ideamapping*, you'll have some solid information to work with. You're now ready to go on to the next phase in the process, "writing" the speech. Please note that we put the word *writing* in quotation marks. You'll soon see why.

Step 3

Assemble the Pieces and Parts of Your Speech

"If you would persuade, you must appeal to interest rather than intellect."

—Benjamin Franklin

Step 3 Assemble the Pieces and Parts of Your Speech

3.1 Let Your Fingers Do the Walking: Information Gathering

After you do Ideamapping or outlining, you begin the process of gathering information. Just what kinds of information do you need for this presentation? The list below is representative of some of the resources you might need to consult in order to flesh out your ideas for the speech or presentation.

- **Budget information**
- **Statistics**
- **Quotes from articles, books, internet, experts**
- **Quotes from your president or other company resources**
- **Your own experience or anecdotes from others**
- **Other items**

You can see that this part of the planning process is interesting because it's here that you conduct your research. Depending upon the nature of the speech: formal versus informal, technical versus non-technical, long speech versus short, you'll have to decide exactly what information is necessary and how much of it you'll need.

It's also at this stage that you begin to consider what visual aids might make the most sense. (You'll find details about using Visual Aids in Step Four.)

Gather More Than You Need

It's always best to gather much more material than you'll need. Remember, one of the most frightening things about public speaking is the fear that someone (or worse, everyone) in the audience will know more about the subject than you do. This fear of "being found out" causes more speaking anxiety than any other. As we've previously mentioned, the way to avoid the fear is to *over-prepare*. We've said that it takes one hour per minute preparation time. Here is where the hours begin to add up.

Of course, a lot will depend upon how much you already know about your subject. If it's a type of presentation such as a sales forecast or a quarterly meeting speech that you give often, the amount of time you must spend to get ready will be reduced. When you're preparing a whole new speech, be ready to spend significant time in this stage. You'll want to read up on the subject, clip newspaper and magazine articles, check the internet, look at videos, listen to tapes, talk with people—whatever it takes to familiarize yourself with the information.

Creating Folders

It's a good idea to keep all of your data in one place so that each time you have a chance to work on the speech, materials are at hand. We recommend creating separate file folders in some of the following categories:

Folder One: Planning work: Purpose, T-Bar Analysis, Dates, Times, Location, etc.
Folder Two: Related articles & Information from Internet
Folder Three: Statistics, data and note cards
Folder Four: Interviews with authorities or experts
Folder Five: Anecdotes, Vignettes, Jokes & Quotations
Folder Six: Visual Aids & Handouts

These folders are terrific for a couple of reasons. First, this system allows you the freedom to pick up diverse bits and pieces of information related to your topic at various times and store them in a logical place. And, keeping the folders where you can easily see them allows your subconscious mind to go to work on ideas, even when you're not consciously thinking about the presentation.

Keep your working folders near your desk or computer. As you add material to your folders, you'll be building the information base you need to create a great speech.

Using Note Cards

We recommend skimming through books, magazines, the Internet and other sources for your subject and making notes on 3 X 5 cards. A note card might look like this:

Idea: Outsourcing training
Article: Business in the 90s, Funny Management 6/98 p. 27
By John Smith
Larger companies are outsourcing 30-40 percent of training.
Smith's Quote: "The trend in outsourcing is going to redefine business."

Gather as many note cards as you need. As you go about preparing the speech, you might want to separate the cards you plan to use for this speech and put them in the number 3 folder. Keep others you've written up in a file box for some future speech or for an article that might come out of the speech. Once you've completed the speech you're working on, you should place the cards you've used in the file box. We're great believers in using information several times and in several different ways.

What's Your Comfort Zone?

How much backup material do you need to be credible? It depends, of course, on the topic, the audience, and the length of the speech, but in general, you should gather enough information to make you feel comfortable. Each person's comfort zone is unique. For some, a few items are enough, for others, a mountain of material does not give them comfort. Be practical. First decide how much time you'll have to make the presentation. The time you have available will always be the first cut.

The second cut is to consider what type of presentation the audience expects from you. If you're making an academic speech to a group of professors, your style and presentation will be far different than if you're making a speech to the local Chamber of Commerce or if you're presenting a new product line in your Conference Room. Each is important, just different.

3.2 Small Group Business Presentations

Most business presentations are made in-house to people you know and work with on a daily basis. You might be asked to present budget information, a monthly update on a new product line, report on activity in your territory, or any number of other subjects that people get together regularly to discuss.

First, figure out how much time you'll be allotted for your presentation. If you've been given 20 minutes, plan to stay right on time. You'll be noticed for your professionalism if you do. Next, it's important to prepare adequately for these meetings. Often the regularly held meetings trick you into thinking you don't have to spend much time planning. It has been our observation that this might be a mistake or, at the very least, a tactical error. We are not suggesting that you go overboard in preparation, but that you do spend some time getting ready. How many times have you been in a company meeting when the people presenting were winging it? Too many. When it's your turn to present your ideas, be sharp. You want to be recognized as someone who is fully prepared and who knows how to make a terrific presentation.

Here are some guidelines to follow for everyday business presentations:

1. **Know As Much As Possible About The People Attending**. It is important to spend time thinking about who's who and how the group will probably respond to your ideas. This little bit of planning will have dramatic results. Use your T-Bar Analysis.

2. **Use Excellent Eye Contact**. This means you want to be sure to include everyone as you speak. If the decision maker is in the meeting, avoid the tendency to speak more often and more directly to him or her than to the others. (We'll go into detail about how to use eye contact later.)

3. **Watch Body Language.** You can usually tell if people are paying attention to you or if they are interested in what you're saying through observing body language. When you see people yawning or closing their eyes for longer than normal periods of time, you are losing them. If you look at someone who has tilted the chair back and seems to be off in a daydream, you can assume this per-

son thinks he or she has heard everything you're talking about before. If you see this, insert a startling statistic or say something humorous to jolt that person back into paying attention. If people begin talking among themselves, it usually means they are bored or not interested in either the subject or the speaker. When you notice this behavior, change your energy level. Become more enthusiastic. Speak louder or speak with greater authority. Of course, all of these indications can be misleading. Sometimes, someone may just be yawning because she's been up half the night with a three-month old infant. Be careful about judging everyone by strict standards of behavior. Begin to pay more attention to body language each time you speak and you'll soon be aware of what is working and what is not for you.

4. **Don't Ramble.** Be precise and concise in your remarks. It is very difficult for someone in a small group setting to concentrate if the presenter is vague or inconsistent.

5. **Use Good Visual Aids.** It's a good idea to keep your visual aids to a minimum for the smaller meetings. You don't want to overwhelm people with 40 or 50 slides even if they look great. You are better off discussing your points and using visual aids to support your ideas rather than the other way around. Have you ever seen someone give a presentation based 100 percent on the visuals? What was your reaction?

6. **Ask for Questions**. In a small business meeting setting, it's usually appropriate to solicit questions during the presentation instead of waiting until the end. This is a less formal approach and helps the participants to track what you're saying and to check understanding. Be sure to listen attentively to questions. Don't interrupt even if you know the answer as soon as the questioner begins to frame the question. Be patient. Wait.

7. **Be Upbeat**. One way to be outstanding in this type of presentation is to be enthusiastic and energetic. Smile often if appropriate. A huge problem we find in small business presentations is the boredom factor. People get bored very easily, especially when the presenter speaks in a monotone voice and shows little or no enthusiasm. Don't be guilty of boring anyone. It should be your goal to be the presenter everyone talks about after the meeting. "Wasn't that a great presentation?" "I cer-

tainly understand why we have to move in that direction." "The time seemed to fly by." "I think we can reach that goal." If people are saying things like this, you've hit a home run.

8. **Sell the Idea.** Suppose you're making a persuasive speech. Maybe you want to convince a group to buy your product, service or idea. During the seventies, Yale University's Psychology Department issued a list of the 12 most persuasive words in the English language. They're still good today. They are listed below. Try to sprinkle several of these words into your speech. You don't have to use all twelve—that would sound like a commercial—but you can choose four or five and then observe the impact these words have on your audiences. We guarantee you'll be pleasantly surprised with results.

Here's the Yale List:

YOU	DISCOVERY
MONEY	RESULTS
SAVE	HEALTH
NEW	PROVEN
EASY	GUARANTEE
LOVE	FREE

Ultimately, the words and visuals you choose are your personal decision, aren't they? We know that the same subject with the same time frames delivered to the same audience will be totally different depending on the speaker. That's what makes public speaking fascinating.

3.3 Out of the Mouths: Strong Openings

Most audiences expect to have ho-hum experiences when they hear a new speaker, and with good reason. Most speakers rely on traditional methods that include easing into the speech with some overused phrases such as "I just want to tell you a little bit about..." Or, "I've been asked to speak about the budgets, and I know this is a dry subject but..."

Or how about this one, "You've probably heard this before, but I just want to tell you about…"

And there's the really old fashioned and, we believe, *wrong* advice to speakers: tell *a joke to begin every presentation.* You might have been advised to use the old "a funny thing happened on the way to…" type of joke. Most of these jokes do not represent the topic and are told strictly to warm up the audience. In most cases, the joke falls flat and the audience is not amused. Why? Telling a joke is an art form. Most of us really don't understand the split-second timing that is required to make a joke work perfectly. Telling a joke that falls flat is fatal for any speaker who wants to make an impact (and we all want to make an impact). Our advice is to avoid telling the latest joke to open your presentation unless you are an absolutely terrific joke teller and the joke has a strong connection to your topic. (We'll be talking much more about the use of humor in your presentation later in this step.)

The openings we've mentioned so far are forced and ordinary, aren't they? Why? They don't offer one single hint of what's to come, of who you are, how creative you can be or how they relate to your subject. If you use one of these openings, your audience will expect an ordinary presentation. This is definitely not your goal. Your goal in the opening should be to let the audience know, immediately, *why they should stop and listen to you now.* If your opening achieves its purpose, you'll actually see the audience shift and sit up, ready to pay attention. When that happens, you know you've intrigued them.

How to "Write" A Superb Opening

How do you begin a presentation that gets immediate attention? Here are some ideas to consider:

1. **Use what is commonly referred to as a "grabber."** This means you want to say something short and evocative that sets the tone and pace of the speech and grabs the audience's attention right away. We recommend that you base your innovative, exciting idea on the final *so that* purpose statement you prepared back in the planning stages. This idea should reflect something about where you intend to go with your presentation. The purpose statement is your reason for giving this

particular speech. To let the audience know what is on your mind right from the beginning does wonders for you as a speaker. The audience tunes in to your thought patterns and is, in most cases, eager to hear what you have to say. Even if the audience is not that interested in a subject, (yes, it does happen), people will be interested in you and how you present your ideas.

People are always fascinated with other people. That's an essential element of life—to begin to understand how others think and act. So, if you're bored or boring, your audience will get that message and the speech will become one more unremembered waste of everyone's time. That's not what you want for yourself. Now, we know that every speech cannot be a barnburner, but every speech can reveal something about you. You owe that to each and every audience and anything less than that shortchanges them.

You know, inside, whether you're giving your all or not. *And every audience knows it too.* You can make a commitment to make every presentation important and worthwhile. If you do, everyone wins, and it all starts with your opening remarks.

2. **The opening statement should be memorized**. Although we are not proponents of memorized speeches, we are in favor of learning *by heart* both the opening and the closing. Since these two parts of the speech are so important, you don't want to leave them to chance. Openings and closings should be very short, from a single word like "Wow!" to three short sentences at most.

3. **Use a question to provoke audience interest**. Many speakers open every speech with a question because it's an easy way to get started and to gain audience interest. The question you ask is generally a rhetorical one so you're not expecting a response from anyone. The question is used to set the tone for the speech. For example, a speaker might say, "Are you happy with your child's teacher?" Or, she might say, "Are you living the life you dreamed of as a child?" Or he could start with, "Have you become part of the wacky world of the Internet yet?" Each of these questions sets a definite idea in motion.

4. **Start with a short quotation.** The quotations should capture the essence of your speech. Short quotations can be very effective tools to help an audience focus on your ideas. It's important that you memorize the quotation so you can say it right into someone's eyes as you begin your presentation. *Bartlett's Familiar Quotations* is a great source and there are many other anthologies of quotations from writers, philosophers, and politicians to current movie idols and sports figures. Today you can find thousands of quotations on computer software programs as well as in your local library.

In addition, you can find great sources in your daily newspaper and weekly and monthly magazines. For example, *Reader's Digest* prints great little sayings that can be wonderful for openings. And don't forget to listen to the children in your life. They often have magnificent ways of describing their world. Try to capture the innocence of their worldview. Audiences love these little stories and vignettes.

Here are a few examples:

For a speech on the power of imagination. John Dewey said, *'Every great advance in science has issued from a new audacity of imagination.'* I love the idea of audacity...to me it means letting go and letting your brain run wild. Do you want to be audacious today?

For a speech on kids who return home to live after college. Robert Frost must have been thinking about my family when he said, *'Home is the place where, when you have to go there, they have to take you in.'* because my 23-year old is back home and most of her friends are back home, too. Kids seem to be returning home after college at record speed. What's going on?

For a speech on the need to change. Heraclitus understood the dynamics of change when he said, *'You can't step into the same river twice.'* Yet we all know that change is inevitable. I know. I lost my job ten years ago and it changed my life.

You can see how you can weave all kinds of information into the opening of your presentation to make it stand apart from the ordinary. That's the goal—to say something new and interesting so the audience sits right up and says "This speech is going to be worth hearing."

5. **Use a startling statistic**. Audiences love to hear statistics that prove a point quickly. The key word here is *quickly*. You don't want to paralyze an audience with numbers and charts that are long, complicated and difficult to grasp. In the opening, you want to use your startling statistic to drive home the purpose of your presentation.

   Here are a couple of examples:

   Did you know that 87 percent of CEOs say that communication within the company is the biggest problem they face? 87 percent! I work with CEOs pretty regularly and they just can't understand why this is such a huge problem.

   Third quarter profits rose a whopping 28 percent. We did it! Let's celebrate!

6. **Use a Visual Aid.** You can easily grab attention by using a visual aid or a prop of some kind in your opening. The prop could be a hat, a costume, a baseball, a bowl of spaghetti, or any number of things that would tie in to your presentation. You might consider doing a quick demonstration if it will capture your audience's interest. Jessica uses a baby doll as a prop to talk about The Signals of Communication. We saw a speech once where a man had a glass of water and a pill. He took the pill very slowly before he started speaking. Then he said in a powerful voice, "Miracles do happen. I am lucky to be alive today." Imagine the impact on the audience as he unfolded the story of his near-death experience.

Examples of Grabbers

Here are some opening grabbers we've used in our speeches and seminars:

Jessica: "Life is about communicating and babies know it. (She holds up a Coochy-Coo doll.) They cry (press tummy and doll cries) and coo (pat and doll coos) to get our attention and it works. But life goes on and crying and cooing doesn't cut it for most of us."

Dorothy: "How many of you love to speak in public? How many hate it? The hates have it. We're going to try to swing that vote today and get you to move at least to the *like* stage."

Jessica: I once started a presentation on the differences between internal and external promotions by putting up a slide of a belly button. I let people look at it for a few seconds and then I said, "There are innies and outies and we need both. The same is true for sales promotions."

Work It Out

Here's a chance for you to practice writing a "grabber" for a presentation or speech you're working on. Let's try several approaches, just to give you some practice in thinking about great openings. Try to put your own personality into the opening.

1. **Write an opening posing a question.**
2. **Write an opening using a startling statistic**
3. **Write an opening using a short quotation**
4. **Think of a visual aid or prop you could use.**

Remember to tie the opening to the purpose of your speech. And also aim for brevity. The best "grabbers" are short and to the point so the audience knows it is in for something different and interesting.

3.4 Shut Thy Mouth: Strong Closings

This is a good place to talk about your closing statements since the same rules apply for the close as the opening. You'll want to say something dramatic, or at least interesting, when you reach the end of the speech. It is unnecessary to say something like, "In conclusion" or "In closing I'd like to say...." These introductory closing comments are similar to the weak openings we mentioned at the beginning of this chapter. What you need at the end of your presentation is a tie-up statement. You want to say or do something that the audience will remember long after the speech.

Here's your chance to summarize your main theme so it is clearly embedded in the minds of the audience. Take a close look at your Final Purpose Statement as you prepare your close. You should find the idea you need right there. You might want to use a startling statistic or a question or any of the other ideas we mentioned for developing the opening. Go for a real sense of closure rather than just drifting off.

Your audience must know when you reach the end of the speech that you've tied all of your ideas together into a neat, cohesive package. The closing must make absolute sense to the audience as a natural outflow of the subject itself.

There is some argument about whether the speaker should say *Thank You* at the end of the presentation. While at Confidence Builders we are well known for our manners and courtesy, here's one place where we feel strongly that saying thank you at this point tends to weaken the power of the speech. You want the audience to reflect for a second or two on what you've just said. The *thank you* at this time dilutes the speech because it usually sounds like a cliché rather than a heartfelt statement of how you really feel. Of course, it is perfectly appropriate to say thanks when your host returns to the platform or at some later time.

What should you do the second you are finished with the speech? PAUSE. Do not say a word and do not move an inch. Have you seen speakers who finish a speech and then immediately run off the stage as if to say, *"Whew, I'm glad that's over"*? Sure you have. Or have you watched speakers who finish the speech and then fall right into a totally different voice pattern, and different posture and appearance? This makes the speech itself seem out of context with reality. We recommend that you pause for at least five seconds at the end of your speech. The pause is essential to let the audience know that you are in complete control. And remember to maintain eye contact. Look out into the audience during the few seconds of silence. This will create a strong connection to your audience. It's powerful. (You especially want to be silent while the audience is applauding.)

If you're planning on holding a question and answer session, after you pause, come out from behind the lectern if you've been using one. This is the time to smile at the audience as if to say *I'm finished with the formal part of the presentation, and I'm ready to let you ask questions.* (We have good information about how to handle Q & A sessions in Step Six: Making A Great Speech.)

3.5 Shaking the Skeleton: The Key Idea Outline

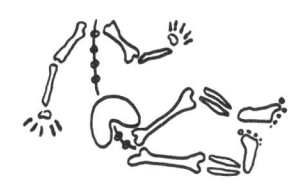

How do you move from point to point effortlessly? People who attend our Confidence Builders seminars want to know how to go about building a speech that works for them and appeals to the audience, too.

It's time to look at the body of the speech. Some call it the heart, the body part that pumps life into the speech. It's time to put some meat on that skeleton.

Do you write a full-length script for your speech? We say an emphatic NO. Still, some people find the only way to get ready for a speech is to write the first draft out completely. If that's what you need to do, by all means do it. However, you might want to try our suggested method just to see if it'll work for you.

Using A Key Idea Outline

A Key Idea Outline is the best way to capture the information you want to use. After you've completed your Ideamap or Roman Numeral Outlining, and information gathering, it's time to prepare your Key Idea Outline. Rather than trying to write complete sentences, which you are likely to forget when you're up there speaking, write only the *major idea* to trigger thoughts. Keep it simple. Use one word or a short phrase to capture each main idea. You are learning how to speak extemporaneously. Remember we said that speaking extemporaneously means a speech that is previously planned with few or no notes. This means you do not want to memorize anything other than the short opening and closing.

The key idea outline represents a road map of your ideas, but *each time you rehearse the material, your words will be slightly different*. And that is exactly what you want to happen. You're not trying to say specific words, you're trying get concepts and ideas across. This will make a huge difference in the quality of your speech.

It is true that you must do considerable rehearsing to reach your comfort zone, but we believe it will take far less time than the amount of rehearsal you'd need if you decided to write out and memorize a speech word for word.

Elements of a Key Idea Outline:

1. **Write out the opening line(s) completely.** Do this just in case you forget your opening in the heat of the moment.

2. **Use thick or heavy paper for the outline.** Heavy paper helps avoid that crinkling sound when you handle it. Write in big, bold letters so you can simply glance down at the paper and easily see what you've written.

3. **Write down key idea words or phrases only.** No sentences. If you write a sentence, it's likely you'll want to read it. Reading is not your goal.

4. **If it will help you relax, you can draw a smiley face to remind you to smile more often.** You can also mark times when you should pause, but don't become too mechanical or the speech will suffer.

5. **Write the complete closing statement**. Keep it short. This is for your comfort zone. You can go to the close at any time—for example if you find you are running out of time, go directly to the close.

SAMPLE KEY IDEA OUTLINE:

Dorothy:

This outline is one I used for a 2-hour presentation on Coaching for a banking organization. Notice the print is large and bold and black. I write my outline on what is sometimes called Oak Tag. It's a heavy weight paper—almost the weight of cardboard. I use these because they do not bend or crinkle and they are easy to handle. I number each page so, in case I lose my place, I can easily find which page I'm on.

ASSEMBLE THE PIECES AND PARTS OF YOUR SPEECH

1

OPENING: The IQ of a team is higher than each individual on the team. We're going to raise the IQ of your team by helping you become great coaches.

Create—planning stuff

Organize: Winnie the Pooh story

Attract: Interviewing techniques

Communicate: Do Positives

Help

2

Expect

See What teams want

Communication: Paper Exercise

Eye Contact & Smile Stats

CLOSE: The IQ of each coach here is higher now! Be a great coach. Make your people great! You have the tools. You can do it—I can see it in your eyes!

Simplicity is Key

Notice that the words and phrases in the Key Idea Outline are very direct and very limited. You don't want to write sentences (except for opening and closing). Why not? All you want to see when you look at this outline is a trigger. A **trigger** is a word or phrase that creates an avalanche of thoughts about a subject. For example, in Dorothy's Key Idea Outline, she used the words: **Organize: Winnie the Pooh**. This simple trigger will lead her to share the definition of organizing as proposed by Winnie the Pooh.

Dorothy will be able to spend at least one minute on this idea because she knows what she wants to say about this management concept. The words will also lead her to use her overhead transparency or computer generated image with a picture of Winnie-the-Pooh and the definition on it. You can see that each key idea triggers a whole series of thoughts around that subject.

The nice thing about using a key idea outline is that it is so easy to see. You can place your outline on a table or a desk and, since the letters are so bold, you can quickly glance down and pick up the idea. No squinting or trying to decipher handwriting.

Jessica's Method:

Jessica uses the large index cards. For some reason she prefers the color purple. Here is a sample of a Key Idea Outline she used for an 8-hour presentation on our program called **SIGNALS of Communication.**

OPENING: Life is about communicating. Babies know it. They cry and they coo to get our attention, and it works—(Baby) they know exactly how to communicate, don't they? What happens as we get older?

Objectives

Great Communicators

Paper Exercise

Positives

Superior Attitude—Smile Stickers

Inferior Feelings—Eye Contact/Pacing Exercise

Gender Differences

Authority Figures—Dorothy Story

Listen—6 1/2 Steps

Listening Exercise—Magazine

Likeminded Behavior

Top Ten—Self Awareness

Posters

Wrap-up

Closing: Let's get back to our baby (hold up) I challenge you to find the natural communicator in you.

3.6 Tickle Their Taste Buds: Anecdotes and Stories

When You Want to Make Your Speech Spicier

What is an anecdote? It's an amusing or interesting story or tale that puts people, places, and things into real-life situations. You should add anecdotes as the spice in your speech. Some people think they'll have a hard time telling a story in the middle of a factual speech about an engineering problem, or when presenting the details of a thorny accounting situation. As a matter of fact, most speakers don't tell enough stories, yet it is through the art of story telling that people begin to relate to your facts as well as to you as a speaker.

For example, if you're trying to tell an audience that new layoffs are due to a downturn in profits for three quarters in a row, you can tell them the facts alone...the statistics that drive the decision to lay off a certain percentage of the staff. Your presentation will be much stronger and much more believable if you can weave a story or two about how these layoffs are going to affect actual people.

For example you could say,

I know how you must feel at this moment. As I look out among you I see Tony Finelli. Tony, you've been with this company for 17 years now and you know how hard this step is for us. We can promise each and every one of you one thing—as soon as the situation returns to normal, every single person who is affected will be called back. We need you. We'll come back from this. I know we will.

By doing this, you create a scenario that people can put themselves into. And, while it does not make the news any easier to absorb, there's something credible about a speaker who understands that this speech is not just about cold, hard facts, it's about how people are going to feel about them.

Of course, not all anecdotes and stories relate to hard times. The best stories are the kind that tell personal incidents that lead to discovery of some universal truth understood by everyone. For example, you can get great ideas for a story line from American poet Robert Frost's poem, *The Road Not Taken*.

> *"Two roads diverged in a wood, and I—
> I took the one less traveled by,
> And that has made all the difference."*
>
> —Robert Frost

Here are the ingredients for a really good story. A character gets to a fork in the road of his or her life and has to choose one path or the other. The consequences can be life altering. Almost everyone has had to reach a tough decision at some point in life, and sometimes they choose the right path for themselves and other times, they don't. In either case, there's a great story for you to tell. Can you think of one right now?

Dorothy's Story:

My father, Jim Sanders, and his younger brother, Olen, were two eager young men from Texas who wanted to stake their claim in life. They knew they'd never find their fortunes in the small Texas town where they were born, so they hitched a ride to Chicago, Illinois in February 1927. Although they fell in love with the glamour of that best of all mid-western cities, they knew right away that the cold, windy winters would be too hard on two Texas boys.

They decided to flip a coin to choose their destiny. Heads meant they would go to New York and Tails meant they would go to Los Angeles. Before they flipped, they agreed they would both abide by the decision. My father flipped the quarter and it came up Heads. The young Texans were on their way to New York City. They arrived in New York with very little money and lots of ambition. The two brothers lived the rest of their lives as New Yorkers and never regretted the decision based on the flip of the coin. But sometimes in quiet conversation, my father would wonder aloud, "What would my life have been like if the coin had come up Tails?" I know one thing for sure. I wouldn't be here to tell this little story.

The professional speaker/storyteller, Grady Jim Robinson, says in his book, **"Did I Ever Tell You About the Time..."** that what he calls Relationship Speaking usually works best because "the primary purpose is to break down the natural barrier between speaker and audience...the professional speaker's intention is to make the deepest emotional connection with the audience, a connection that invites the participation, emotionally and physically, of the listener."

How Many Stories and What Kind Will Work?

Where To Find Stories

Stories are like wild flowers on the roadside, you can pick them up and create beautiful bouquets to share.

The first place to look for a good anecdote is in your own life. Your life is full of little incidents. Just think back to this past week. Didn't some funny things happen to you? Some sad things? Did you get some shocking news? Did something unusual happen? Or did the same old thing happen? That's a story in itself.

One of the best ways to always have a fresh supply of anecdotes is to keep a daily journal. In the journal you record the little events of your life along with the major life-changing things. We like the idea of a *daily* journal because it helps you capture the mundane, but interesting things that become the parables for life. Great insights often come from small moments. Life is lived in the details, and people love to hear small stories because they can identify with them and with you. Use them in your speeches and presentations and see what happens. You'll be pleasantly surprised—and so will your audiences. They'll see you as a real person, not just someone with information to share.

How Many Stories Work In A Speech?

Sometimes people ask us how many stories they should use in a speech. Bill Gove, now in his late 80s, still an active professional speaker and one of the founders and the first president of the **National Speakers Association** headquartered in Arizona, says we should build what he calls vignettes one upon another to create the speech itself. In a twenty minute speech there might be as many as fifteen vignettes. A vignette is a short sketch. All of these vignettes are used to create an atmosphere. The stories are presented as a series of bridges that tie together the overall theme of the speech.

We love anecdotes or vignettes, too. There is no magic formula we know of that you can use in preparing a speech, i.e., a ratio of stories to facts. Just know that a speech with no stories is dry and uninteresting. A speech that is nothing more than a string of unconnected stories is incomprehensible and irritating to the audience. Consider balance and you'll choose just the right number and the right stories.

Ever Feel A Knot in the Stomach?
Here's A Tip to Save Your Speech When All Else Fails

If you're ever in the middle of a speech or presentation, and the audience seems to be losing interest and you're suddenly developing a knot in your stomach because you don't know what to do, try this *surefire* idea. Simply say these precise words:

"Now I'm going to tell you a story."

Say the sentence in a softer voice than your usual one. You want to say it as if each person in the audience will be the only one to hear it...sort of a secret between you.

Here's what will happen—an immediate hush will fall over the room as they wait to hear your story. In the total silence, you've got their complete and undivided attention. Now it's time to tell one of your stories. You'll have hundreds of stories (or at least tens) to draw from because you're going to start gathering stories starting today, right?

As you go through your story or anecdote, modulate your voice from time to time—go louder for emphasis or softer to make a point. Remember how important the voice of the storyteller was when you were a kid? That's the feeling you want to recapture. Your story will help the audience relate to you. There's nothing like telling a story to reveal something about yourself.

You'll be pleasantly surprised to find out how well this technique works. It proves that people love to hear stories. Give them what you know they love and you'll become a more successful speaker. Your stories don't have to be spectacular or mythological. Just use material from your own experiences or anecdotes you've heard from your parents, grandparents or friends. Stories, vignettes, and anecdotes offer fabulous insights to help people follow your ideas as you make the presentation or speech.

One Note of Caution:

Before you tell one of your stories you need to spend some time fine-tuning it. If you try to tell the story "cold," it will be too long and it will usually contain too many details. What you want to do is either write or audiotape the story so you can see it written out or hear it. You'll probably find that you're saying or writing such things as, "Well, it was around noon, or maybe it was after lunch when I..." Or, you might say, "There were three people standing on the corner of Main and Vine that day and as I walked down the street I saw my old friend, Stuart, darting across the street..." Unless the three people are important to the story, leave them out. By practicing and listening you'll keep the best parts and let go of the details that detract from the story. You want your stories to sound smooth and easy to follow so everyone gets the point immediately.

Work It Out

Here's an opportunity to capture a story or anecdote on paper. You'll be gathering lots of them from now on, but for this exercise, please think back to an incident in your life you'd like to use in a future speech or a presentation. This story can be humorous or sad, exciting or ordinary, from childhood or something you just experienced yesterday. Write it out in rough draft form first to get the flavor of the story on paper. Then you're going to edit the rough draft to make sure the story will fit into the time frame usually allotted for a speech.

Let's agree that your story should be up to and no more than two minutes. Edit the original until you think it will take up to two minutes to tell. Then say it aloud to hear how it sounds. Finally, do a mini-critique. Does the story work? Did you place the right emphasis in the right places? Can you use this story in a real speech or presentation?

You have five tasks:

1. **Write a rough draft of a story or anecdote**
2. **Edit the story**
3. **Say the story aloud**
4. **Critique the story (What effect will it have on the audience?)**
5. **Say the story aloud again (rehearsals work)**

You should have come up with a short story that will be yours to tell the next time you need it. People love story telling. It goes back to childhood. Stories represent magical moments to most people, and they will listen. Remember to use the exact sentence, *"Now I'm going to tell you a story."* It sets the mood for the story to follow. This little trick works wonders and you'll have your audience ready and eager to hear what you have to say about your main topic.

3.7 Belly Laughs and Silly Grins: Jokes & Humor

People love humor. Period. Nothing sells a speech more than a great sense of humor. We're not talking about telling the latest joke or an old joke that's been around for years. The kind of humor we recommend for a speech is based more on using anecdotal material and story telling than on joke telling.

As we mentioned earlier, telling a joke is an art form. Split-second timing is required to make the punch line work. Unless you are known as a great joke teller, don't try one in your speech. It is almost guaranteed the joke will fall flat on its face. That is not what you need to build your self-confidence as a speaker.

If you've ever heard someone tell a joke that didn't work, you know what we mean. The silence that follows is painful! It's difficult to recover from a bad joke. Once a joke fails, people will be listening to see if you're going to attempt to tell another joke—and they'll be watching to see if you fail again.

Does this mean you should not attempt to use humor? No, not at all. There are many forms of humor, and telling jokes is only one of them. Most of the time it's best to leave the jokes to the pros. Let them take the chances with audiences. That's their profession. You don't have to put that kind of pressure on yourself unless you know you're really good at it.

Dorothy's Story:

I did a series of presentation skills training classes for a Fortune 500 company in New York. One of the participants was a vice president of marketing named Jack. Jack was a good-looking man of about 50. When we talked about the class, he told me that his biggest problem was that he could get through a presentation with no problem, but as soon as he sat down, his whole body began to shake. It was a delayed reaction to the nervousness he felt during his presentation.

I noticed that one of the things Jack always did was tell a joke at the beginning of the speech. His timing was just a little bit off, so the punch line almost worked, but not really. When Jack sat down after his practice presentations, he began to shake badly. It was very noticeable to everyone in the class.

*As we discussed the problem, it became clear to me that Jack had convinced himself that he had to become **a professional comedian** every time he spoke. The idea of competing with the pros simply scared Jack to death. He was putting way too much pressure on himself. Once he learned that he did not have to tell a joke to start each speech, he relaxed and his body tremors went away forever.*

Humor Everywhere

> *"The human race has one really effective weapon, and that is laughter."*
> –Mark Twain

Often, the best humor is the kind that's directed toward what's happening in the moment. For example, good speakers are extremely aware of everything that's going on in the room. If something is out of place or odd, the pro can spot it and make a comment about it. A person who feels uncomfortable as a speaker will not be able to take advantage of the noises and intrusions and just plain funny things that go on during any speech or presentation. The lights may flicker. Great chance to make a humorous comment such as "Oh I guess they forgot to pay the light bill." The audience loves this ability to grab a situation and make the most of it. If someone drops something and it makes a loud noise, you can stop and acknowledge it in some way. Or if someone sneezes, take a second to acknowledge it. People appreciate the fact that you're really present and aware of what's happening.

Being in the Moment

Jessica's Story

You never know what's going to happen when you're making a speech. When I worked for GECC, I was making a presentation in Nashville, Tennessee with a co-worker. We were at a convention for riding lawn mowers and there were about 600 dealers in attendance. We were doing a skit about selling mowers using our financial methods. I was a very inexperienced speaker at the time and was playing the part of Minnie Pearl buying a lawn mower. Well, someone inadvertently leaned up against the wall in the back of this huge convention center and all the lights went out. It was pitch black. It only took a few seconds for someone to figure out what had happened and the lights were back on. My choices were to ignore the situation or to acknowledge it. As soon as the lights came back on I faced the audience and, in a voice I didn't know I had, I yelled out, "WELL HOWDEE!" The crowd roared and we went back to our presentation.

How to Use Humor In Your Speeches

1. Never make fun of anyone in the audience.
2. Find everyday stories that relate to your topic.
3. Seize moments of humor during the speech and include them.
4. Never use ethnic, gender, or off-color humor.
5. Use self-directed humor.
6. Smile often.

Be A Humor Magnet

Humor is all around us. We simply need to become humor magnets. Before we can use humor effectively, we have to be able to see it in everyday things. Make it a habit to listen for humorous stories or vignettes. Have you ever waited on line at the grocery store? Some funny things happen there. What about the times you're stuck in traffic. How do people react? What about the dentist's office? Or how about kids? Kids can provide mountains of stories because they are always doing or saying the unexpected.

It's usually an unexpected turn of events that makes a great story. Sometimes an incident doesn't seem funny at all when you're actually experiencing it, yet in the retelling, you can begin to see the humor. These are usually wonderful stories since they have high levels of personal intensity, and they make you more "human" to your audience. And that's the key idea: you want to be able to share your own mistakes and vulnerability with the audience because when they hear your story they identify with one of their own. Your story helps them realize that they are not alone and that other people have done stupid and silly things, too. The laughter of recognition is the best kind. It creates a bond between you and the audience. And each time you tell another story, the bond grows stronger.

Think about some of the stories you've heard or better yet, lived, that can be translated into funny anecdotes or vignettes. To find what's funny in life you simply have to be aware of people and events.

Dorothy's Story

> *I was shopping one day in a grocery store in Philadelphia. An elderly couple stood behind me at the checkout counter. The woman turned to the man and said, "Did you get a head of salad?"*
>
> *I thought the expression was terrific, so I used it in one of my writing seminars to describe how people use our language in interesting ways.*

Work It Out

Stop everything and think funny. Come up with one funny incident in your life and write it down. You know, the kind of incident that made you see how humorous life can be, even in the most serious situations.

You have 3 tasks:

1. **Write out the funny incident in full detail.**
2. **Edit the incident to fit into the format of a speech or presentation.**
3. **Tell the story to someone, see if they laugh with you.**

Now you have a humorous incident to add to your growing list of anecdotes and stories.

Be a Good Humor Man or Woman

For people who do feel comfortable telling jokes, there are books and magazines out there filled with jokes and stories for speakers to use. If you find one that fits your topic and your personality perfectly, rehearse it. Try it out on friends and family to gauge reaction. If they laugh and like it, you can use the joke, but only if you feel totally at ease. Never force a joke. It won't work.

You might want to try keeping a humor logbook. Every time you come across a story you think you might be able to use, write it in your humor book. It's amazing how quickly you'll fill this book, and it will serve as a wonderful resource for you every time you speak.

> *"Take time to laugh—
> it is the music of the soul."*
>
> —ANON

Jessica:

> *I keep a manila folder on my desk where I put humorous items I've clipped from magazines, etc. When it's time to make a speech, I pull out the folder to see what fits.*

How about finding someone to share humor with on a regular basis? You and this person might agree to meet once a week or once a month to share the stories you've found. Try them out on each other and see where the laughs are. This would be a great and productive way to spend time and it would help both of you to develop your funny side (everyone has one, although sometimes it seems pretty well hidden).

> *"Smile—it's the second best thing you can do with your lips."*
> —ANON

What about the simple act of smiling? Isn't smiling a form of humor? It's amazing to us to see how many people give a presentation and never smile—not even once! Smiling is hard to do when you're feeling nervous or when the butterflies are flying around in your stomach. We have a startling statistic to share. We read in *Men's Health Magazine* that children tend to smile on average 400 times a day! Isn't that a wonderful statistic? And grown-ups smile an average of 15 times a day. (that's honest smiling, not the phony smiling we do so often during the course of a day.) Let's think about this disturbing number. What happened between childhood and adulthood? Why is it so hard to relax and smile?

W.C. Fields said, *"Start every day with a smile and get it over with."* Of course, that was vintage W.C. Fields. One of the things we can do is to practice smiling *more* often. If we'd add 2-3 smiles each day, we'd be ahead of the game. Imagine what would happen with your speeches if you chose to smile several times during the time you have available? There would be an incredible difference in how you'd feel and how the audience would react to you. Smile—it's free and worth the effort.

A last thought before moving on. If you can get the audience to lighten up through laughter, smiling, or even a simple grin, you are well on your way to making a stronger connection. According to Daniel Goleman, author of **Emotional Intelligence**, *"Laughing, like elation, seems to help people think more broadly and associate more freely...the intellectual*

benefits of a good laugh are most striking when it comes to solving a problem that demands a creative solution."

At Confidence Builders we live with the principle *Laughter Precedes Learning*. If you want someone to learn or at least to open up and listen, get him or her to laugh a little first. Well-placed humor is one of a speaker's most valuable tools.

> *"A smile is an inexpensive way to improve your looks."*
> —Charles Gordy

3.8 Build that Muscle: The Body of the Speech

As you are building the speech or presentation, you'll want to go back to your original Key Idea Outline to begin to select the precise information you plan to use in the body of the speech. For example, if you wrote in the original outline that you were going to talk about marketing plans for second quarter, now is the time to choose the precise ideas you want to convey in the presentation. The Key Idea Outline is the original road map you've produced to help you go through your major points logically. Most speakers choose to highlight the major point first and work down from there. You may recall that we recommend that you only work with 3 major ideas. Now is the time to explode those initial ideas into detailed explanations.

Whatever your general topic it's up to you to decide how you're going to present your ideas. For every major point you want to make, ask yourself the following questions:

1. What is my opinion or position on this subject?
2. What facts and figures do I need to substantiate my position?
3. What anecdotal material can I find to emphasize the point?
4. What reaction can I expect on this point?
5. What kinds of visual aids will be most effective to make this point?
6. Is there a place for humor in this section?

7. Is this an emotional issue? Will it raise doubts or fears?
8. What kinds of questions can I anticipate?
9. Do I have enough or too much information on this point?
10. Will the timing work?

If you focus on answering these questions, you are bound to build a great speech. Once you've completed this section, you'll be ready to plan for your visual aids. Before we take a look at the various types of visual aids you can use, take time now to make a mini-presentation. You've been studying hard and it's time for a pleasant break. Just follow along with the next **Work It Out** exercise. You'll enjoy this one.

Work It Out

Here's a valuable exercise called the two-minute profile, which we use in all of our seminars on public speaking. If you can find a couple of other people to share this experience with you, that would be great, but you can easily do this on your own. If you have a video camcorder, this is the time to get it out and use it. If you don't, try taping the exercise on your audiocassette player.

A great way to get started on any new program is to stop and think for a minute about who you are today and where you've been thus far in your life. The idea behind the two-minute profile is to ask you to think back to a story or anecdote from your life that has nothing to do with your current career or job. We'd like you to think of an incident from your life that is funny, dramatic, or heartwarming.

Take a few minutes to jot down some notes about this incident and then stand up and deliver your two-minute story. You can do this alone or you can have an audience. The point is to get you to speak about someone you know intimately—yourself. The story you choose will be right for you because it belongs to you and to you alone.

We always do this exercise in our Confidence Builders seminars and we've heard some wonderful stories—funny, sad, poignant, and sometimes bizarre. Here's one that sort of fits the poignant category. A vice president of one of our client firms shared this anecdote at one of our team building seminars.

One Man's Story:

I was raised in a small village in Argentina. When I was six years old, I had a canary for a pet and every morning it was my job to feed and bathe my canary. I loved to do it. To bathe the bird, I would put water in my mouth and let it spout out and over the canary's feathers. One day, I used too much water and the canary drowned right there in my little hand.

You can imagine how devastated I was, so my mother took me by the hand and we went into the village to buy a new canary. We selected one that looked just like the first and as we were walking home, I felt very nervous about carrying the new bird so tightly clasped in my hand. I kept holding the bird tighter and tighter and tighter. When we got home, I opened my hand and the little canary was dead! I cried and cried.

Imagine the effect this story had on the participants. Here was a strong-willed vice president who was a no-nonsense executive. After he told his story, the people in the group saw him in a decidedly different way. Here was a real live flesh and blood person with strong emotions. The other executives began to talk to him in a different way. We experienced a paradigm shift that day.

Jessica's Story:

My sister and I are two years apart. When I was around 10 and my sister Robin was 8, we played a game called Waitress. We waited until everyone else went to bed and then we'd start the game. The object was to sneak into the kitchen and make something really creative for us to eat. The person who had to make the snack was called the Waitress. The other person was the Customer who waited eagerly in our bedroom. Being the oldest, I always said, "Robin, you go first." And she'd always fall for it.

Robin was and still is extremely creative. She'd make these marvelous concoctions and we would happily eat her creations. Then she'd say, "Okay, it's your turn." My response was always the same. "Oh, I'm so full, I couldn't possibly eat another bite of anything." And it went on like this for a couple of years. I never played Waitress. And Robin doesn't let me forget it.

Of course, when you tell your story, be sure to fill in the details to expand it into a two-minute mini presentation. We've heard stories about high school antics, honeymoon mishaps, and all other sorts of anecdotes that warm the heart.

Here's why this little exercise can be helpful to you. Telling a story from your own experience will do wonders for you as a speaker. You'll find that it's easy to tell and that you're not at all nervous telling it. It will be relaxing to you and put you in just the right frame of mind about public speaking and how to make it one of the most rewarding things you do.

If you have a camcorder, by all means, tape your story to see yourself as you present it. If you have a tape recorder, tape it and listen to yourself. This should be the real you, the one you're searching for as you get up to speak in a real-life situation. And if you have an audience, please ask for feedback. Find out how your story was accepted. Find out as much as you can about how you appeared (relaxed, animated, etc.). Have fun with this assignment. It's meant to help you see what a good speaker you already are.

Your Two-Minute Profile

> Please jot a few notes to help you prepare a two-minute story based on something that has happened to you. It could be a funny event, an eye-opening experience, or a story about something that changed your life. Remember this is for **two minutes only** and it cannot be about your business life.

Was it fun? We hope you enjoyed the memory and the experience of sharing a personal story.

Step 4

Tackle the Details

"If you care at all, you'll get some results. If you care enough, you'll get incredible results."

—Jim Rohn

Step 4 Tackle the Details

4.1 Out of Body Experiences: Why Visual Aids?

It isn't always necessary to include visual aids in your presentations. It's up to you to decide if adding a visual component to your speech will make it better, more exciting, or more appealing to the audience. Sometimes you want the focus of attention to remain on you, with no distractions.

We believe the decision to use visual aids or not should be based more on the subject itself than any other consideration. If you have an important announcement to make, you may not want to use visuals because you want complete attention focused on you. But if you are introducing a new product or a new concept, visual aids will enhance your presentation considerably. So there are no hard and fast rules other than good old-fashioned common sense and some pretty startling statistics.

> We remember
>
> > 10 percent of what we read
> >
> > 20 percent of what we hear
> >
> > 30 percent of what we see
> >
> > **50 percent of what we see and hear**

If you choose to use visual aids, there are many types available to you, from simple flip charts to the most sophisticated multi-media extravaganza. We're going to focus mostly on the simple, do-it-yourself type of visual aid. There are wonderful professional organizations available to help you with the big stuff.

Let's start with a basic premise. There is a huge clue in the words themselves—*visual aid*. The clue word is AID. The main point is that you never want to overpower your speech with visuals that speak louder than you do. A visual aid is there to bolster your ideas, to show pictorially what you are expressing verbally so that the audience gets two views of the same idea: your words and the visual representations of your idea. You never want to be subordinate to your visuals. Have you ever seen this happen with a speaker? We have and it seems unfair to the speaker and to the audience.

One of the first things you need to know as you plan for your visual aids is the size of the room and the number of people you expect to attend. We'll start with the small conference room where many of you will be making your presentations. Usually 10-12 people can sit comfortably around a table in a conference room. What is the appropriate type of visual for this room configuration?

You have a couple of choices. Let's say you choose to work with a flip chart. A flip chart is one of the most common and easiest to use visual aids. You'll need lots of paper and good marking pens. We like the colored marking pens that have a good broad edge so you can make your letters large and bright. Some of these pens are scented, and that's an added bonus. We like the black one that smells like licorice.

10 Guidelines for Using A Flip Chart

1. **Use Block Letters Only**. Script writing is very difficult to read, so avoid it for flip charts. You want to write in bold, strong strokes so your words are clear.

2. **Use Key Words or Phrases Only.** Keep it simple. A flip chart is not meant to be used to write complete sentences. Sentences are too hard for the audience to read and follow. It's your responsibility to dramatize your ideas with key words or simple phrases. And you must be aware of your spelling. When someone notices a misspelled word on your flip chart, it's not only embarrassing, it makes you look unprepared or less than professional.

3. **Use simple drawings or stick figures.** Sometimes you can drive home a point with a little cartoon or a quick pie chart. With a flip chart, you want to keep everything simple and direct—don't get carried away with the artistic renderings.

4. **Lettering should be one inch high for every fifteen feet.** You can see that if you have a large room, a flip chart might not work simply because the lettering would be too hard to see from the back of the room.

5. **Use color for excitement and emphasis.** Our studies have shown that color excites the imagination and, perhaps more important, aids in memory. So if you want your audience to remember your points be sure to use a variety of colors. You can use color dramatically to highlight a point as you discuss it or to check off a point you've just made. This makes the visual aid more exciting to the audience. It is a simple, yet effective technique.

6. **Use lots of white space.** Don't try to crowd too many thoughts on one page of the flip chart. The general rule is the eye can absorb only **13 lines** of copy *including* the white spaces.

7. **Don't apologize for your art work.** Just assume that everyone will "get" what it is you're trying to convey. The easiest way to accomplish this is for you to explain what the diagram or artwork represents, *without apology*.

8. **You can prepare in advance.** There might be some ideas you want to write out ahead of time and turn to at the appropriate time in your speech. If you choose to do this, be sure to give yourself ample time to create your "masterpieces." You don't want to be working on them as the audience is beginning to arrive for your presentation.

9. **Write as you go.** It's fun to write as you go. As you reach a major point in your presentation, you might want to illustrate it on the flip chart. One piece of advice: NO EYES, NO TALK. When you are writing and looking at the flip chart DO NOT TALK! Wait until you've finished and then turn to the audience and talk. If you talk while you're writing, the audience feels left out. Once you have written the information on the flip chart and you refer to it, use the old-fashioned but still useful **Touch, Turn, Talk** method. That is, you Touch the words you're highlighting, Turn to face the audience, and then Talk. This is an old rule but one that works.

10. **Keep it Simple.** Flip charts are perfect for creating simple visual demonstrations. Make use of the immediacy of the flip chart to help your audiences follow along with your key points.

Some People Are Very Happy With Overhead Projectors

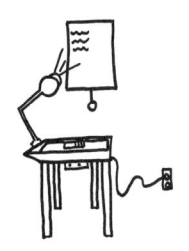

One of the advantages of using an overhead projector is that the room can remain well lighted and that helps sustain audience interest. Another advantage is that you can use this medium effectively for either small groups or larger ones (up to 200 people), so it's versatile.

Transparencies are relatively easy to make: they can be made by hand or with a computer program such as Microsoft's Power Point. Lettering on transparencies should be at least 1/4 inch high (30 points). It's a good idea to do a rough drawing of how each transparency will fit into your presentation before you actually produce it. You want to have a style that follows through from beginning to end. For example, if you choose a border, it's a good idea to be consistent with that border. Since transparencies can be made in horizontal or vertical shapes, choose one or the other and stick with it for the whole presentation. It looks amateurish to switch back and forth. You want the visual aspect of your presentation to be just as professional as you are.

The brain is excited by color, so it's to your advantage to use it in your transparencies to help your audience absorb the information quickly and easily. However, try to use colors wisely. You don't want to confuse the audience with too many colors on one transparency. Planning in advance will help you control a tendency many people have to overdo, especially with the new computer programs that allow us to add colors with one key stroke. Moderation is probably the key idea here. Have fun with your colors, but don't go overboard.

Be sure to mount your transparency on a frame. This is professional looking and it also helps for transporting and storage. And, another side benefit—you can make pencilled notes on the frames for easy reference during your speech.

It is absolutely *unnecessary* to have an overhead transparency for every point you're making. We've seen speakers show up for a speaking engagement with a transparency for every sentence. This is overkill. Select key ideas only, the ones you know the audience needs to see on screen. It's much more effective to be minimal in the use of visual aids.

Turn off the overhead projector after you've made your point. You want to leave the transparency up only long enough for everyone to make notes or to get the idea. Then, turn off the projector until the next time you plan to use it. No one wants to stare at a visual that refers to something you were talking about ten minutes ago, or worse, to look at a blank lighted screen.

One of the nice things about the overhead projector is your ability to create transparencies during your presentation. You can use blank transparencies and write on them with markers, or you can write with the markers on your prepared transparencies to point out or highlight specific numbers or words. There is a nice sense of immediacy and control in being able to do this. Be sure you've practiced the technique before you try it in front of a live audience.

You want to be sure you know how the projector works, how far it needs to be from the screen for the best effect and how to focus it. Setting up usually takes at least 30 minutes, so please allow this time for yourself before you have to get up to speak. It will increase your comfort zone and that's one of the tricks all professional speakers know—the greater the comfort zone, the better the chance for a successful speech.

What if you're not the only speaker on the roster? What if you are scheduled to be third or fourth? Please don't wait until the last minute to arrive for your portion of the presentation. If you can be in the room while the person preceding you is speaking, you'll be able to see how the audience is seated, how the overhead slides look, if the room seems warm and so on. Unfortunately, you might not be able to do much at this point to change the environment, but it is better to be aware of what's happening than to walk in cold and not have a feeling for the situation.

If you do get to a speaking engagement only to find that there is no overhead projector and your whole presentation is based on using slides, what do you do? Do not panic! There is usually nothing you can do if there's been a mechanical failure or if the equipment you need is just not available. You have to deal with the situation you are given and still go on and be brilliant. The audience must never know you've been blindsided. That's why we're going to talk about the value of rehearsal time. A great speaker is ready for any and all emergencies.

Computer Generated Presentations

Computer generated presentations are the most exciting new form of visual aid and we predict this medium will have the greatest impact on the way presentations are delivered. You can create fabulous presentations with software programs such as Microsoft PowerPoint 2000, Lotus Freelance Graphics, or Corel

Presentations 8. Today it is possible to create your presentation, save it, add to it, delete outdated portions, make it in color, animate it, use sound—the list of advantages goes on and on, and the future promises unbelievable advances in this kind of software.

As people become more and more computer literate, they will be able to create dynamic presentations that will be breathtaking for audiences because of the capability inherent in this most modern media. It is now *relatively easy* for anyone to learn how to create computer presentations; however, the old adage "a little knowledge is a dangerous thing" might be applied here. One problem we have seen is the overuse of the medium. Since it is so easy to add gimmicks, we're finding that some speakers are overdoing the use of graphics, animation, and clip art. We want to remind you that *less is more*—especially when you're trying to get a point across. Make the slide glamorous, but keep it simple.

According to John Byrd in his article for Delta Airlines' **Sky Magazine**, *"It's the Software, Stupid,"* presentation software is becoming more and more sophisticated. He says "just because a program gives you 30 different special effects, that doesn't mean you have to use all of them, or even one."

You can use a monitor for your presentation if the group is very small or you can have several monitors placed strategically around the room for larger audiences. Many speakers prefer to use a big screen for larger audiences.

The downside of computer generated visual aids is the technology involved. There is always the possibility of Murphy's Law going into effect—*whatever can go wrong will go wrong*—and when that happens with a computer, it's difficult to recover.

Jessica's Story

> *I was invited to attend a training and technology seminar sponsored by a visual aids technology company. At Confidence Builders we had been thinking about ways to improve our presentations through technology, so I eagerly accepted the invitation. Imagine my surprise when the meeting was held up "due to technical difficulties."*

Once the demonstration actually got started, the projector quit working and the presenter had to call the office for assistance. I was shocked and disappointed. Technology is a great tool for presentations. Preparation is key. Everyone needs to have a backup plan ready to go into action to avoid a disaster similar to the one I witnessed at that unfortunate Technology Seminar.

Videos & Movies

Audiences like to see videos if they relate to the subject. Be sure to strategically place enough television monitors around the room for viewing ease. It's also a good idea to keep the videos relatively short. (About 20 minutes works)

Sometimes just a clip from a movie is great to show to make a point. Be sure to check copyright laws before showing movies or videos. Since current audiences are so used to watching videos, movies, and television, your video must meet very high standards to compete. And always check this medium out before you show it. We've seen speakers stranded when the video just didn't work. This creates an embarrassing moment for everyone. Also be sure to check the equipment. VCRs and movie projectors are notorious for breaking down, or for needing just the cable you don't have available. If it happens that your equipment does not work, don't panic! You must be prepared to go on without the medium. Don't over-apologize. Just get on with your presentation. This is a good time to inject a little humor. The worst thing you can do is to pretend nothing is happening!

Jessica's story:

Recently I was doing our SIGNALS of Communication program for one of our clients. As I was reciting the TEN COMMANDMENTS OF GOOD LISTENING, I got to number four, which is Remove Distractions. At precisely that moment, unknown to me, an audiovisual technician walked into the room behind me and started rummaging around for something in the closet. The audience started laughing and I didn't know why. I continued on to the next commandment—number 5— Show Empathy. The technician shouts out, "Yeah like don't laugh at me." I turned around and saw him for the first time! It was a priceless moment in training. We all laughed for quite a while. I couldn't have planned it better.

Models & Objects

We saved models and objects for last because sometimes a presentation works better if we go back to the "Show and Tell" mentality we learned in elementary school. If you have something that people can see and touch, taste or smell, bring it. There's nothing like having the thing itself to make a point. If you choose to allow people to handle the object, allow time for this because you don't want the model to become a distraction as you continue to speak. If the audience is large, you might want to simply show the model and ask people to come up to see it after your presentation.

You Have a Variety of Options:

Plan to use visual aids if they will enhance your presentation. With so many options available, you should have no trouble selecting the ones that are right for you and for your speech.

It's important that you feel totally at ease and comfortable working with the medium you've selected. If you are going to use some piece of equipment that is new to you, please give yourself adequate time to become familiar with which buttons to push and so on. You certainly don't want to *practice* in front of your audience.

When Do Your Hands Hand Out the Handouts?

To keep your audience informed and involved both during and after the session, you might want to offer some written reference materials.

The audience likes to have written material to help follow along with your presentation, to make notes, or to refer to at a later time. You should consider what best serves your particular audience's needs. In our Confidence Builders seminars, we provide 3-ring binders with our 6 1/2 Step course materials inside. These are actually working documents, so notes are taken and kept in the binder.

Most participants keep the binder on a bookshelf, which serves to remind them of what they've learned in the seminar. We also do a lot of live videotaping in our Public Speaking seminars and each participant is given his or her tape to take home for review.

Decide early on what kinds of materials (if any) make sense for your presentation. You may want to prepare something as simple as a one-page key idea outline with space for note taking. Or you might have a brochure or pamphlet you'd like each participant to have. Speakers debate about when to give the audience written material. Some say it is distracting if the material is handed out before or during the speech. Some speakers feel that too much of the speech will be revealed in the handout, thereby losing the element of surprise.

Others say it lends credibility to have the material available from the beginning. These speakers feel that retention of the information will be enhanced if people can see it as well as hear it. Whichever way you choose to handle the distribution of handouts, be sure that each piece of paper has your name and phone number on it. This is a great form of advertising—the handout becomes your personal calling card.

A word of caution:

Audiences love to find errors in your material. It's that *I gotcha* syndrome that some people find exciting. Be sure to edit and proofread every document very carefully. It might even be better to have someone else do it for you. Your reprints should be crisp and readable. Use lots of white space to make the documents easy to read. Your credibility is on the line when you speak and when you hand out material that supports what you say. There is no room for error.

Another word of caution:

If you plan to distribute your handouts *after* you speak, please tell the audience at the beginning of your speech. People hate it when they try hard to keep up with a speaker's ideas by scribbling notes as fast as they can, only to find that the ideas are already printed on a handout. A new idea we endorse is to tell people that they can get an e-mail version of the handout if they want it. This is a great paper saver.

A final caution:

If audiences plan to take notes, tell them to take the "Aha" type of note only. It's not usually necessary to write down every idea a speaker shares. An "Aha" is an insight that has special meaning to an individual. Each member of the audience will have different "Ahas." For those who like to do Ideamapping, here's a perfect place to use the technique. It's a great way to take notes.

Remember, visual aids and handouts help you get your points across more dramatically and often more effectively. As you plan your presentation, take time to consider what kinds of visual aids or handouts will make the greatest impact. Don't forget, though, you should always be the primary visual.

4.2 Off the Top of Your Head: Creating Titles

You might consider doing a quick Ideamap to come up with a good title for your speech or presentation. The title is important because it attracts audiences and it also foreshadows the flavor of the speech. A title such as **Effective Business Writing** says something quite different than this title—**Caution! Words at Play!** The audience will expect the first speech to be relatively dry and business-like and the second to be more humorous. You don't have to go for humor, but you should try to come up with a title that is catchy and beyond the ordinary.

For example, how do you respond to these two speech titles?

1. **Real Estate Markets in the Present Economy**
   How to Make a Fortune in Today's Real Estate Boom
2. **The Problems of Employee Turnover**
   Why Good People Leave Great Jobs—What You Can Do To Make Them Stay

Notice that the first title in each case is too generic. The titles leave the audience wondering just what will be covered in the presentation. It's perfectly all right to use the words "How To" and "Why" as part of a title if you plan to reveal the answers in your speech.

Here are some examples of speech titles we've used:

Oops! Your Attitude is Showing!
All Aboard the Communication Line
How to Have Fun With Your Body Parts
How to Get the Decision Maker to Stop, Look & Listen
Put the *Sizzle* in Your Presentation

Work It Out

Let's practice creating a few titles. We'll give you a generic title and you come up with something more specific.

Generic Title: **Retirement Can Be Fun**

Specific Title: _____

Generic Title: **Team Building for the 21st Century**

Specific Title: _____

Generic Title: **The Personal Computer and You**

Specific Title: _____

Did you think of some interesting and provocative titles? You can see it's important to focus on specifics so the audience will know what to expect. Are you working on a speech right now? If so, why not do an Ideamap to see if you can come up with a couple of titles that reflect what you want to say.

Work It Out

Do an Ideamap for a title. This should be quick and fun.

4.3 Should I Memorize? (We Wish You Wouldn't)

Remember this?

Extemporaneous: Previously Planned, But Delivered With Few Or No Notes

The difference between memorized and extemporaneous speaking is vital to you as a speaker. If it seems we're harping on this idea, we are. Remember we said earlier, when you deliver an extemporaneous speech, you have spent just the right amount of time preparing it, using the key idea outline. When it's time, you get up and say the words that are on your mind and in your heart. **This is the best way to give a speech.**

You are totally prepared because you know precisely where you're going from point A to point Z. You've rehearsed and you've done all the things we've been talking about in this book to get ready for the speech...but you have not memorized the words. That bears repeating: **You have not memorized the words**.

Your words come from the experience of the moment. And that's thrilling. You feel energized because you are actually *living* the speech as it happens, and your audience is excited because every audience knows immediately if a speaker is truly present or is stuck on memorized words. Audiences appreciate speakers who know the speech well enough to deliver it without notes—or with just a few notes.

When you deliver a speech you've written out word for word and memorized, here's the problem—you might forget a word or a line. What happens then? Most people panic! We've seen it happen often. A speaker is going along just fine with the speech and suddenly a startled look comes over his or her face. It is at this precise second that everyone in the audience knows what's happened—a lapse in memory. At times like this, the speaker wants to die and the audience squirms a little. Within seconds the speaker finds his or her place, but the *magic* is gone. Everyone knows that from this moment on, they are in on a contest to see if the speaker will remember the rest of the speech. The focus shifts from the strength of the speech to the fragility of the speaker.

The solution to this problem is the **Key Idea Outline** we've recommended. It is simple to do and it saves you from potentially embarrassing moments. Basically, it allows you to plan and rehearse your speech, not worrying about the precise words you'll say during the speech—knowing that the perfect words will be there when you need them. If this sounds difficult to you, it's probably because you can't imagine the panic you'd feel if you knew you were going to stand up in front of an audience and let the words simply take care of themselves. It's amazing, but most people who use this method report that they feel calmer and more sure of themselves when they rely on a key idea outline rather than a memorized speech. Try it for yourself.

Dr. Wayne Dyer, in his book **You'll See It When You Believe It**, says, "I do not use notes when I go before an audience...when I gave up my attachment to perfection about speaking, paradoxically, a kind of perfection seemed to enter into my performance on stage." Dr. Dyer makes hundreds of presentations each year with no notes.

But What If I Absolutely Must Read My Manuscript?

What should you do if you just have to read a manuscript? Sometimes you must present facts and figures or legal information that has to be delivered exactly as it is written. Here are six recommendations for those times when you must read your speech:

1. **Write the material yourself.** It's tempting to allow a speechwriter to provide you with a manuscript. The problem with this approach is that it's usually obvious to the audience that the words you're reading are not actually your own. Each of us has a particular style and cadence, we have a rhythm and a jargon that identifies us. It's our *speaking signature.* If you must use a speechwriter, be sure he or she listens to you speak several times to try to determine your personal speech patterns and to insert these into the speech. Our bottom-line advice is to write (or at least rewrite) your own speeches.

2. **Practice, Practice, Practice.** Mark the places where you tend to stumble over words. If you hesitate or stumble over the word or

phrase more than once, consider getting rid of it. It's obvious those words do not fit your personal style. Remember that there are limitless ways to get an idea across. Don't be afraid to discard anything that seems hard for you to say.

3. **Make the manuscript easy to read**. Double or triple space and use a larger than usual type size—-go from a 12 to a 16 point if you have any trouble seeing. You'll feel more at ease knowing that you can see the words clearly.

4. **Mark the manuscript up.** Underline key words or phrases for emphasis. The manuscript represents your personal comfort zone. It should contain everything you need to feel comfortable when you're standing up there speaking.

5. **Read and Look. Read and Look**. The best way to read a manuscript is to look down at the script quickly and silently. Then look up at someone in the audience and say what you've just read. Repeat this process throughout the speech. This is a difficult discipline and requires a great deal of practice, but it can be done. The worst thing you can do is to look down and read the whole script and, in a sense, forget about the audience. You've seen speakers who do this and you know it doesn't work. If you should lose your place, don't panic! Simply stop and look for it. It's amazing, but audiences are people—they understand!

6. **Ask for questions.** It is important to include a question and answer session at the end of any presentation in which you've had to use a manuscript. Why? You definitely want to show your vulnerability and accessibility. Once you've finished the formal portion, say something like, "I'm sure you have some questions." or "I usually have a lot of questions about this subject." At that point, step out from behind the lectern. It's important to physically move away from the lectern because you want the focus to shift from the message itself to you. Now the audience will have a chance to find out more about you and your ideas. Let your answers flow, without notes or charts. Now it's just you standing there, willing to share ideas. Don't miss this opportunity to connect with your audience.

4.4 Using A Teleprompter

We have a story for you from Dorothy's daughter and Jessica's sister, Robin Albritton. Robin owns a company in Houston called *What Are You Looking At?* She is an expert on the computerized teleprompter that so many speakers use today. Here's what Robin says about how to be effective using the teleprompter.

"A teleprompter is a valuable tool for speakers. The speaker actually reads from a computerized script that appears on a screen. The words are scrolled across the screen, a few at a time, at a pace the reader can follow.

"When every word is important, for example at a Stockholder's meeting, or when you're videotaping for company-wide distribution, it can help your presentation if you use a teleprompter. After all, reaching the audience is the primary goal of any speaker and if using a teleprompter can help you do that, by all means use it.

"The teleprompter professional is there to help the speaker. Since using this sophisticated equipment can be frightening, I recommend rehearsing a few times before the actual speech to get a feel for the rhythm of the words as they scroll by. It's sort of like reading the words on a Karaoke screen. The person working the prompter is a professional who knows how to help you do your best. Be willing to work with him or her. If you're taping, know that tape is cheap and you can do many takes to get the words right for you and your style.

"Most people who use a teleprompter for the first time develop a real case of stage fright. They don't understand how the equipment works and they don't like the feeling of being out of control. When you use a prompter, don't be afraid to ask for help.

"Many of my clients are CEOs and senior executives. They have people on staff who write their scripts. The executive shows up for the speech. The script has been typed into the teleprompter. In some cases, the script doesn't quite fit the style of the executive, so rewrites and changes have to be made on the spot. This is part of the teleprompter professional's job—to be able to accommodate to change quickly and efficiently."

Quick Tips for Working with a Teleprompter

Here are Robin's tips for working with a teleprompter:

1. Know your topic

2. Rehearse two or three times

3. Read script conversationally

4. Look right at the teleprompter as you speak

5. When you are finished reading, hold eye contact for at least 4 seconds

6. Be committed to using the medium and learn how it works

4.5 Rough Drafting

It's time. You've come a long way and now it's time to actually work out the first "rough draft" of the speech itself. Notice we put the words rough draft in quotation marks because we want to again caution you that it is not necessary to write down a whole script for your speech. What you're looking for at this point is a carefully thought out key idea outline with the details you think you'll use in place.

For example, if you have chosen a great anecdote to illustrate a point, you should have it clearly in mind and you should have a good idea of where it belongs in the speech. You insert a word or two in the key idea outline to let you know this is where you think this anecdote should go. The same is true for any visual aids you plan to use. Note where these will appear in the outline. Some people even write words such as SMILE and PAUSE at appropriate places to remind them to do these things.

Your goal now is to formulate the real speech, from the written opening through the outline to the written closing. Here's an example of the rough draft of a key idea outline:

Key Idea Outline (Before Final Edit)

Title: OOPS! Your Attitude is Showing!
Overhead: Oops! Your Attitude is Showing!

My Opening:

"7 seconds—-that's all you get to make an impression. 7 seconds.

Let's count it out together. One thousand one, one thousand two, one thousand three, one thousand four, one thousand five, one thousand six, one thousand seven. Not long to decide how you feel about someone is it?"

List 6 1/2 Signals
O.H. List of Signals
O.H. Great Communicators
Oprah story
Attitude Studies—use Ben Franklin quote
O.H. Positives
Gender Stories: driving/dinner
Smiling Stats
(Pause) Give out Smile stickers
Closing: So think about how many 7-second chances you still have to make a great impression. Don't forget "Oops, your attitude is ALWAYS showing."
(Pause & Smile)

Work It Out

It's time for you to create your own Key Idea Outline. Take your time with this.

Think about your *so that* formula and your T-Bar. Consider your opening and closing. Then decide the sequence you want to follow. Organize your thoughts so they flow easily from idea to idea. Here's where you want to insert your anecdotal material. Jot down an idea that will help you recall the story or stories you plan to use. You might also consider what visual aids you plan to use.

You're beginning to get a picture of how the speech or presentation will go.

Key Idea Outline

Now that you've completed your own Key Idea Outline, we're ready to look at what's been accomplished so far in our one hour per minute journey to an excellent speech.

4.6 Sit On It: The Power of Editing

"If you want me to talk for ten minutes I'll come next week. If you want me to talk for an hour I'll come tonight."
—Woodrow Wilson

You have a speech. Congratulations!

Are you happy with it? The next stop along the way is to do a final edit on what you've completed so far. By now you should have gathered statistics, anecdotes, humor, and ideas for visual aids. You have your rough draft key idea outline ready. You might even have a working title for your speech.

Now, before you actually rehearse the material, take a few minutes to make sure you're satisfied with your progress. Each step along the way to a great speech requires some looking back before going on. It's time to take an objective inventory of what you've developed so far. You want to fine-tune the key idea outline so you're sure you feel comfortable with the material you're using. You don't want to memorize words or to write a full-length script.

This is the time in the **6 1/2 Step ANATOMY** of a speech when you begin to speak your ideas *out loud* for the first time. Of course, the first time you try to vocalize your ideas, they'll sound awkward and you probably won't like the result. But here's the payoff: you will find, as you rehearse, some wonderful treasures hidden in the speech that you'll definitely want to keep and other ideas that just don't seem to work. Toss these now.

Editing is about taking an *objective* look at the speech. It's at this point that you step away from your creative side and take a cold, hard look at your creation. It's time for your left brain logic to kick in and go to work for you.

A Few Tips for Editing Your Speech

1. **Sit on it**. After you've gathered all the material you need for the speech, leave it alone for a while. That is, literally walk away for a short period of time. You've probably gotten too close to the material to be objective. After a break, you can come back and hear and see the speech in new and different ways. We recommend overnight if that's possible. At least give yourself an hour's break time before beginning the editing process.

2. **Say the speech aloud** and tape-record it. There is nothing quite like hearing your own voice. You must know how you sound when you speak. If your voice is shaky or high-pitched, you can do deep breathing exercises to change this characteristic.

3. **Listen to the tape for *content*.** Focus on ideas and how they flow from point to point. Don't worry too much at this point about *how* you present. Think about *what* you are trying to get across. We'll focus on style in a little while.

As you listen to the tape, ask yourself these questions:

- **Is my opening provocative and interesting—A Grabber?**
  Is it related to the purpose?
  Refer to the *so that* Formula

- **Have I made my 3 key points?**
  Refer to the left side of the T-Bar Analysis

- **Have I considered my audience?**
  Refer to the right side of the T-Bar Analysis

- **Do I have enough anecdotes & humor and are they appropriate?**

- **Will my visual aids work?**
  Are they easy to use? Interesting?
  Do I have enough? Too many? Will I use them as handouts?

- **How's my timing?**

- **Do I have a strong closing?**

- **Do I like what I have so far?**

4. **Place an asterisk on your key idea outline next to the really strong points** you hear on the tape. You want to make sure you don't forget these because they work to make the speech a good one.

5. **Be ruthless** about getting rid of extraneous material that does not add to the total concept you're trying to get across in the speech.

6. **Let someone else listen to the speech**. Explain that at this time you're only in the editing stage, it's not really a rehearsal yet. Ask the person to listen only for content and the flow of ideas, not style. Incidentally, select someone who will give you honest feedback. You know your friends will say, "It's great," just because they are your friends. You need the truth.

7. **Time the speech**. Start to get a feeling for how much time you'll need to make your points adequately and to use your visual aids. In most cases, you'll find your timing is off—sometimes overextended by as much as half the time you have allotted for the speech. That means, if you have 20 minutes, you'll find that

you might have at least 30 minutes worth of material. This is all right at this point. Now is the time to think about what needs to be cut or pared down. *Preparing a speech is a process of change.*

8. **Make the necessary changes.** In most cases you'll be deleting material to fit into your time frame. However, sometimes you'll find you have to add an anecdote or a new visual aid to drive home a point. And here's your opportunity to change priorities. Often, when we hear our speech spoken, we realize that the most important point is hidden somewhere in the middle of the speech, so we need to move that point to the beginning of the speech.

9. **Now it's time to create your final key idea outline.** This is the one you're going to work from as you rehearse and the one you'll use when you actually make the speech.

10. **It's important to be satisfied with your presentation at this point.** You don't want to overedit. Remember there is no perfect edit; therefore be willing to let go. You've done your homework.

Those 20 Hours Are Adding Up

Now you're beginning to see why it takes 20 hours to prepare a 20-minute speech! But the work is fun and rewarding. When you get up there to speak and you feel totally prepared and comfortable you'll feel great about the time you spent getting ready.

Last Minute Jitters...

You're almost there—the speech is ready. You're ready. There are still a few things to think about before you actually deliver the speech. Don't get discouraged now. You're about to become a great speaker. And if you're experiencing any last minute jitters, that's normal. One sure sign of a growing awareness is when you feel as if, instead of getting better at a task, you're getting worse. Remember when you learned how to drive a car? Just before you felt fully competent, there was a moment when you thought you'd never get the hang of it. That's probably where you are right now in your quest to become a great speaker. Hang in. Your hard work is about to pay off. First, we need to focus on some important external details.

4.7 Location, Location, Location...

Location is important to a speaker. For example, if you're used to making presentations in your small conference room and your boss tells you at Monday's staff meeting that you'll be the keynote speaker at your company's national association luncheon meeting for 1,000 people, first you'll need to take a deep breath. Then you'll need to find out as much as you can about the facility, the agenda, other speakers, and what is expected of you. No need to panic. Let's walk through this scenario together.

Where Will the Speech Be Delivered?

Let's say your annual meeting is being held at the luxurious Boca Raton Hotel & Club in South Florida. The date is February 10. (This can be a nice perk, especially if you're from Minnesota and the snow is three feet deep in the month of February.)

If you are lucky enough to pull this kind of an assignment, plan to enjoy every minute of it. You certainly don't want to spend your time worrying about the speech itself. All your preparation will have been done well in advance. You know the speech will go well so you might even plan to spend an extra day just soaking up the South Florida sunshine. Wouldn't that be a treat?

But what if your presentation is right in the conference room of your office or at the local hotel? In any case, it's important to check out the meeting room space *in advance* if that is possible for you. You'll want to see the actual room in which you'll speak, check out the seating arrangements, check out where you'll be when you're speaking, the visual aid equipment such as an LCD or VCR and the general ambiance of the room itself.

Getting to Know the Room Before the Presentation

We like to get to the scene of the speech early, very early. That is, we like to be there with plenty of time to spare. We don't want to come running in at the last minute and be surprised at what's going on around us. One way to avoid becoming nervous is to stake out the place you'll speak early in the day, or in the case of an early morning speech, the night before.

Now, some people may find it odd, but we think rooms have *personalities*. As soon as you enter a room, you'll get a feeling for it. Some rooms are "user friendly." You immediately sense that you're going to be fine working in this room. There's something about the size, height, colors, and seating arrangements that come together to make a room comfortable for a speaker—or uncomfortable.

As soon as you enter the space, you'll know. If you feel the room is not "friendly," and you've arrived early enough, you can begin to make some changes. You can do something as simple as bringing in a green plant to soften the look of the room, or you can change all the seating if it doesn't appeal to you. Often the lighting is wrong for your type of speech. You can have that changed quickly too.

Check the temperature in the room. You don't want it to be too hot or too cold; however, our studies have shown that a cold room is better than a warm one. When the room is too hot, people really become uncomfortable and the attention span wanes considerably.

The responsibility for climate control may seem to fall to someone else, but the fact is that when you're up there speaking, everything is your responsibility. Audiences expect speakers to take complete charge, and they are disappointed when anything goes wrong—disappointed in the speaker, not the meeting planner. Remember this the next time the flip chart pad is empty. Your responsibility. The coffee is not on time. Your responsibility. The pens don't work. Your responsibility. We could add more, but you get the idea. **While you are on stage EVERYTHING is your responsibility**.

Where Will the Audience Sit?

If you have control of the meeting, one of your decisions concerns seating arrangements. In general, the more formal the meeting, the more formal the seating arrangement. If you want people to feel they are in a learning environment, it's okay to set up in a classroom style. In this arrangement, people sit behind desks or tables, just as they did in school. You, in effect, become the teacher. That's the perception you're looking for—teacher/student.

If you'd like your audience to learn in an open and fairly freewheeling environment, arrange the tables in a U-Shape. This works well for up to 20 participants. Everyone can see everyone else easily, and that leads to higher group participation. You stand and speak from the open end of the U. This is our personal favorite meeting room set up for training because it allows us to walk into the U and to come face-to-face with the people. This U-Shape set up is informal and personal.

If your speech is being made to a large group (usually 100 or more) chances are the audience will be seated theater style. This seating arrangement is the most formal and can create a barrier between the speaker on a stage, usually behind a lectern, and the audience, seated at some distance from the speaker. Take great care in these situations to close the gap as much as possible. This can be achieved through body language such as smiling and great eye contact with individuals in the audience.

If you speak to large groups, please be sure to have a lot of appropriate anecdotes to share. Remember, audiences love to laugh. Give them what they want and you'll be a hit. You might even get a standing ovation. Wouldn't that be something? The next time you speak it could happen to you. There's no feeling quite like the one that comes over you when you do get a standing ovation.

Dorothy's Story

A few years ago, I had the privilege of being in an audience of some 3,000 at Philadelphia's Academy of Music. Among the roster of speakers were Wayne Dyer and Deepak Chopra. Even though the crowd was enormous and the seating was obviously theater style, these two speakers mesmerized the capacity crowd. Not a cough. Not a shuffle. The huge audience was totally at one with each speaker. It was as if Wayne Dyer and later, Deepak Chopra, were simply holding a conversation with one or two people.

Everyone in the audience became part of each presentation. It was a thrilling experience for me, and it proved to me that even a room set up theater style can become electrified if the speakers are professional and if they understand how to reach their audiences.

Speaking When Food is Served

If your speech will be made after a breakfast, lunch, or dinner, people are usually seated at round tables of eight or ten. The main problem with this set up is the potential noise level. Often, the audience is being served coffee and dessert while you're trying to deliver your speech. You simply have to learn how to speak through the clatter and hold their attention. *Keep it lively.*

It is especially important if you are an after dinner speaker to make your presentation livelier than usual. People tend to be less attentive right after a meal, especially a dinner that has been preceded by a cocktail hour.

On these occasions, we recommend that you limit the amount of time you speak, use more anecdotes than usual, and try to involve the audience as much as possible. You don't want to lose the opportunity to make a great speech just because you've been selected to speak at a challenging time.

Dorothy's story:

As we write about meeting rooms, one nightmarish occasion pops into mind. We were on the second day of a three-day intensive seminar on management development. Our group consisted of 30 senior managers representing many companies. Each of our speakers was a seasoned professional. Everything was running smoothly and uneventfully when suddenly we heard a trumpet blare. This initial blast was followed immediately by the oom-pah-pah of a marching band! This was going on in the meeting room right next to ours.

I rushed out to find out what was going on. I found out that a major auto dealership was holding a pep rally in the area right next door to ours and they planned to continue the festivities at various times for the rest of the day and again in the morning of the next day. The celebrants were having a great time. I was in serious trouble.

The first thing I did was to call for a refreshment break. Everyone in our group was laughing and wondering what was going on next door. There was no point in trying to pretend nothing was happening! What could be done? I ran to the banquet manager and told him I couldn't believe that he'd booked our quiet little meeting next door to a Pep Rally. Then I heard the worst news—no other meeting rooms were available. Now what?

I ran to find the person from the auto dealership. We sat down together and he understood my predicament. We came up with a solution. He agreed to coordinate the marching band performance times to coincide with extended breaks we agreed to have. Compromise! It worked. For the remainder of the meeting, our breaks began whenever I heard the first trumpet blare. As soon as the band started playing everyone knew it was break time. Our participants decided to make the inconvenience fun, so as soon as the band hit its first note, our trainees jumped up and marched around our little meeting room. They laughed and carried on and had a great time.

What could have been a total disaster for us turned out to be a challenge that led to a lot of fun and good memories for all. It was a stroke of luck that the meeting planner for the dealership was a real pro. He was willing to work with me to make the necessary adjustments to accommodate both of our meetings. Needless to say, we never booked a meeting in that hotel again. They should have had better control over meeting room assignments.

No wonder novice speakers think public speaking is tough. Imagine if this incident occurred during your first speech. The old saying, 'the show must go on' is as true for speakers as it is for actors. Incidents like this happen from time to time and we just have to keep on going somehow.

To Create the Ideal Environment for Your Speech:

1. Provide comfortable cushioned seating
2. Allow adequate space for each participant
3. Use tables if participants are expected to write
4. Provide writing implements
5. Provide name tags and name cards
6. Offer refreshments (when appropriate)
7. Check all equipment in advance
8. Check out the lighting
9. Control the temperature
10. Show that you are in total control and smile a lot!

Dorothy's Story

One time I was making a speech at the South Florida Women's Business Conference. There were over 150 people in the audience. Everything was going smoothly when suddenly a man walked out of a side door and over to the water cooler. He casually removed the empty water bottle and walked out. I didn't say anything because his entrance and exit were swift. Suddenly, the man returned with the new water bottle. He was very slow and casual as he went about the business of replacing the water jug. Now I had to do something because the audience had become fascinated with the water man.

From the stage I said, "Hi. What's your name?" The man turned around and said in a loud voice, "Fred." The audience howled. It was one of those moments that made the speech fun for everyone. Fred finished his task. And as he left, I said, "So long Fred. Thanks for the water." He said, "You're welcome." There was another roar of laughter.

Do you have any stories about your experiences with speaking? If you do, we'd love to hear them and we'll include them in our new books and articles. Just send them to us and we'll even give you published credit for your story. You'll find the mailing address at the end of the book.

Ideal Speaking Environments

As you check out your ideal environment, you'll have to decide where you'll actually stand or sit as you speak.

What's the Difference Between a Podium and a Lectern?

Have you ever stood behind a podium? Probably not. A podium is Latin for a platform or a stage, not that thing you put your notes on and hang onto for dear life. That's a lectern, from the Greek for reading desk. You stand *on* a podium and stand *behind* a lectern.

Think about this—a lectern usually covers almost three-quarters of an average person's body. When you stand behind a lectern, you're hiding most of your body. The good news is that you can look very authoritative—think of ministers and professors. If you want to establish authority, definitely stand behind the lectern. You might want to use the lectern at the beginning of your speech and again at the end, and come out to the side at various times during the presentation.

Some people stand behind the lectern for the whole speech and then come out when they ask for questions from the audience. This shows a certain vulnerability and audiences like that.

The bad news about lecterns is that a lectern can be a barrier to open communication, especially if you happen to be very short or very tall. Today there are electronic lecterns available. You can move them up and down to suit your height, and they come equipped with microphones, computer graphic capabilities, video and sound control panels. Many companies are installing these electronic lecterns in their state-of-the art training rooms. Dorothy has taught writing courses at Dow Chemical. They have a wonderful state-of-the-art training facility in Midland, Michigan and the lecterns are equipped with everything a speaker needs for a great performance.

Speaking of great performances...

Dorothy's Story

Tony Bennett remains one of our most popular singers. He spends several months each year in concert. One of the trademarks of his performance is the solo he does at the end of each concert. There he is, on center stage, with a spotlight on him alone. The rest of the stage is dark. He sings his final song without a microphone! His voice fills the theater. At the end of the song, the audience goes wild with applause followed by a standing ovation. In that huge theater filled with thousands of fans, Mr. Bennett uses his final moments on stage to make a personal connection. It works!

Checking Out the Equipment

1. **Make sure everything works.** Test your equipment before the speech. What would happen if you started to speak and found the microphone was not hooked up properly? How would you feel? Let's remember we're trying to increase our personal comfort zone. Test your laptop and projector to be sure it's working properly, and test the overhead projector to make sure it's correctly focused and that your overhead slides are easily seen from every point in the room. If you plan to use flip charts, make sure there are enough blank pages available for your use. Sometimes you'll want to write your message on the flip chart prior to the speech. Make sure you allow enough time to do this. It seems obvious, but check on the markers you plan to use. Do you like the colors? Are the markers broad-edged so you can make strong bold letters. If you plan to show a video, check out the monitor and the VCR to make sure everything is in working order. And if you plan to do live videotaping, check out the camcorder itself and the lighting in the room.

2. **Find someone to help you.** If you are speaking in a hotel or a convention center, the catering department has people who specialize in helping you set up and check out your equipment. Get the person's name and a beeper number so you can call immediately if anything goes wrong. You can't spend time scouting for help when you're in the midst of your program. If you are speaking in your own offices, there's usually someone on staff who understands the equipment. Make a friend of this person and let him or her know that you will be speaking on a certain day. Ask for help and use it when you need it.

3. **What if equipment breaks down during the meeting?** Stuff happens! If the overhead bulb burns out, stop the proceedings and check to see if there is a spare bulb. It's usually tucked away inside the projector. What if there isn't one? You have two choices. You can go on without the overheads. This is why you absolutely must know your presentation cold. If you've been relying on your overheads to give you direction, you're in trouble. The other choice is to call for a break and then scurry around to see if there is a replacement bulb available in the building. If one can be found, you're home safe. If not, you have to be ready to think on the spot and come up with other alternatives. In either case, a breakdown is something you can expect to happen at least once in your speaking career. (Probably more than one time.) You need to plan for mishaps.

A good speaker handles this and other similar situations such as videotapes that won't work, microphones that screech, or camcorders that don't record, with poise and a good sense of humor. When disaster strikes get the audience involved. The worst thing to do is to *panic*. Audiences are willing to go along with almost any deviation from the norm if they think the speaker is in control. Your sense of presence is critical, especially when things go wrong. You can save the speech or lose it during these critical moments. Save it.

Jessica's Story

Wow! We landed a new client and I was very excited! I'd been trying to work with this client for some time and finally I was hired to teach presentation skills. One of the things we stress in our speaking seminars is being prepared for anything and everything. Normally, I get myself completely ready at home before leaving for the speech. This client was located in a small Ohio town, about an hour's drive from my house. For some reason, I decided to wait until I arrived at the client's to put on lipstick. I parked in the lot with thirty minutes to spare. I reached for my purse. Not there. I looked all over the car. No purse. This also meant no lipstick. So now I had two problems—my lips seem to disappear without lipstick and since this speech was for a large group, I was speaking from a stage with stage lighting. I was in trouble. My face would just fade away.

Okay, I thought, I'll stop at the Gift Shop and buy some lipstick. Here was my second problem. Oops—no purse, no money. Now I had to get really creative. I took out my colored markers and slipped two pinks and a red in my suit pocket. I sneaked out to the ladies room and you guessed it, I colored my lips with the markers. It actually looked good. I had brightly colored lips for the presentation and for the rest of the day. The speech turned out to be fun and the audience gave me a standing ovation. The client gave me a parking pass, so I was able to get home. I sure didn't live with our "be prepared" rule that day. The idea is to be flexible. All kinds of strange things happen when you're a speaker. Be ready and have fun.

So far we've been talking about how to prepare and how to control the environment surrounding your presentation. Next we'll discuss the speech itself.

Step 5

Observe Yourself

"Many of life's failures are people who did not realize how close they were to success when they gave up."

—Thomas Edison

Step 5 Observe Yourself

5.1 Display Those Body Parts: Rehearse

When you hear the word "rehearsal" you probably get an immediate image of actors on stage. Public speaking is similar to acting in that you do stand in front of an audience, all eyes are upon you, and you do perform. That's where the similarity ends.

As you know, plays are written down and actors memorize their lines and are expected to deliver them precisely the same way night after night. This is what the author expects and has every right to expect.

Public speaking is different. You have the opportunity to get up in front of an audience and share *your* ideas. Actors never look directly at the audience because they're in character and the audience is merely a witness to the character in action. When you give a speech, looking right into the eyes of audience members is the vital ingredient that creates interest in you and your ideas. Public speaking and acting have obvious dissimilarities. You are not an actor on that stage. You must be the authentic *you*.

Your rehearsal will be different than an actor's. You're going to try out the speech to find out how it sounds, its content, its pace, its humor or anecdotal quality, and how long it is. Finally, you're going to consider how you feel about the speech and how you think your audience will respond.

Nothing is memorized except the opening and the closing. Everything else is done extemporaneously as you look at your key idea outline to guide you along the way.

Here Is What You Will Need For Your Rehearsal

> Key idea outline with open and close written out completely
> Rough visual aids
> Camcorder or audio tape recorder
> Timer or stop watch

We recommend that you rehearse the whole speech several times. If you have a camcorder, videotape each rehearsal. When you play the tape back, you'll get the most objective view possible, and you'll be able to make the adjustments you need. If you have an audio tape recorder, use it to record each "take" of your speech.

The idea is to be able to go from point to point seamlessly. You want to become totally familiar with the road map, **but not the precise words**. Each time you rehearse, you'll find that you use different words and expressions. That's the way it is supposed to be, otherwise the speech will be "canned." This is not your goal.

When it's time to actually give the speech in front of an audience, your ideas will be completely formed and your choice of words will be just right. You have to trust yourself in this regard. If you rehearse properly, you'll be totally ready to say just the right words at the right time, and the audience will appreciate your natural approach.

5.2 Be Natural, Be Prepared, Be Enthusiastic

There are three things to strive for during the rehearsal and, of course, during the speech itself.

> Being Natural
> Being Prepared
> Being Enthusiastic

All professional speakers know the secret to speaking success is hidden in these three attributes. Let's talk about each in a little more detail.

Being Natural

Allow the true *you* to shine. One of the mistakes we see novice speakers make is to try to emulate a speaker they think is really good. It's great to have role models, but when you speak, you must be totally authentic. Audiences can spot a phony and they don't like it. They feel cheated because they wonder what the real person is like under the façade.

Dorothy's Story:

When I was starting out as a speech coach, I had a wonderful mentor, Charles Reilly, whom we've mentioned earlier in the book. Charlie was like a little Irish leprechaun. He was naturally funny—great with one-liners and quick comebacks. His students loved him. His voice was strong and clear and his humor contagious. The seminar days whizzed by and everyone learned a great deal and had fun.

I, of course, decided this was the way I wanted to be, too. My plan became to watch Charlie, memorize everything he said, and copy his attitudes and gestures. Since I thought no one could do it better, I wanted to become a carbon copy of Charlie.

On my first seminar date, there were eight people in the class. Charlie was sitting in the back of the room, waiting to see his new protégé perform. I was nervous, and although Charlie didn't know it, I was ready to deliver his presentation.

You can imagine what happened. I began to do my imitation of Charlie and the people just stared at me. Here I was a rather tall, elegant looking lady doing a very poor imitation of an Irish leprechaun! I looked and acted like a fool. I felt the audience's eyes on me. Where Charlie was clever, I was stilted; where Charlie was funny, I was awkward. It simply did not work.

Thank goodness Charlie grabbed my elbow at the first break and whispered, "What the h—- is going on!" " I turned to him and said, "I'm doing everything you do." He laughed and said, "Quit doing Charlie Reilly and start doing Dorothy Lynn." He told me I was quite good enough being me!

That was one of the most valuable lessons I've ever learned. In my awe of Charles, I had blinded myself to my own talent. I had to learn that people want to relate to a real person up there. I went back and became Dorothy Lynn again. The material was basically the same, but now I was speaking in my own voice and using my own examples and anecdotes. And it worked.

So, if you think you have to sound like a professional radio announcer or Martin Luther King Jr. when you're speaking, forget it. What you have to do is allow the real you to be there for all to see and hear.

Think of the times you've been in an audience. Do you really care what the person looks like? Do you really care if the person is short or tall, male or female, young or old? Most of time the answer is No.

What you care about most is the person's ability to capture your attention. When it's your turn to speak, just remember the Charles Reilly story. You aren't Charles and you aren't Dorothy or Jessica. You're you and you have earned the right to be up there speaking.

Being Prepared

One of the ways to guarantee your right to speak is to **be prepared.** Sounds like the Boy Scout pledge, doesn't it? Being prepared means that you know your material so well that no one or no incident can cause you to lose your place permanently. It is possible to lose your place momentarily and get right back on track because you know just where you are going.

Being prepared means you'll welcome question and answer sessions because you'll have no fear that someone will ask a question you can't answer. If someone does ask a question you can't answer, you'll have the confidence to say, "I don't know, but I'll be glad to find out."

Guilty as Charged

Is it possible to do a speech if you don't follow the *one-hour per minute* preparation model? Of course. We all do it from time to time. Can you get by? Sure. Do you feel good about it? No, you don't.

People get nervous about speaking because they know they have not prepared adequately. If you know you don't have the facts at your disposal, or if you didn't bother to write and memorize your opening and closing, or to create a key idea outline, chances are you'll show signs of nervousness. You deserve to be nervous!

If you haven't given yourself a chance to rehearse before the speech, you'll be scared. You should be! One of the main reasons people get a bad attack of butterflies is because they feel guilty. They're afraid the audience will see right through them and ask the very question that will expose the fact that they don't know enough about the subject to be up there as an expert.

Spend whatever rehearsal time it takes to feel totally prepared. We use the word "feel" on purpose. You'll know when you are ready. It's that moment when everything fits. You'll feel that you know what you're doing and you'll actually *like* the speech. **Until you like the speech yourself, don't give it.**

The amount of time and effort you devote to preparation depends upon how familiar you are with the subject, the length of the speech, the audience, the visual aids you've selected, and other factors. You'll know when you're ready. When that moment arrives, relax in the knowledge that you're going to give a great presentation.

Being Enthusiastic

> *"Enthusiasm and fear can never share the same stage"*
> —ANON

When you speak, there is no more potent ingredient than enthusiasm! It's the contagious element that is totally obvious to an audience every time you speak. Someone who is enthusiastic shows it with every gesture, every smile, and every word. There is a special attractiveness in a person who looks and acts excited about his or her speech.

Enthusiasm cannot be faked. Sure, we've seen speakers who seem to be wildly enthusiastic, but we can always tell when a speaker is putting on an act. Can you?

The word enthusiasm comes from the Greek, **enthousiasmos**, *having a god within*. The definition includes words such as lively and absorbing interest. That definition leads to some interesting observations. When you are enthusiastic, you are sharing the best of yourself. You've allowed your interest in your subject to become more important than any fear you might have of the audience and its reaction to you. That's when you shine. And you actually shine! Enthusiastic speakers have an almost luminescent quality. Audiences sense it and want to be part of it. You know that enthusiasm, like laughter, is contagious.

> *"Nothing great was ever achieved without enthusiasm."*
> —Ralph Waldo Emerson

How Can You Become More Enthusiastic In Your Speeches And Presentations?

Stop caring more about yourself than you do about others. One of the greatest killers of enthusiasm is personal ego. Your ego will tell you that you are afraid the audience won't like you or your ideas. When ego takes over, honest enthusiasm flies out the window. It's critical for you to stop for a minute and consider that people deserve your best, not because you are trying to impress them, but because you are trying to reach them.

Become deeply involved with your subject. Find out much more than you need to know. A couple of things will happen—your confidence level will go up in direct proportion to how well prepared you feel you are for your speech and your audience will know you're a pro.

Talk about subjects you truly care about. We know it's hard sometimes to get excited about the quarterly report, but it's up to you to find something about your topic that excites you, something you believe in and want to share with others. When you've found the value in your subject, the words will be there and your enthusiasm will be there, too.

Smile a lot during the speech. Even if your speech is on a serious topic, you should smile from time to time because it helps the audience relax and learn, and it helps you relax too. Smiling is good for everyone's invisible body part—the soul.

Pour yourself into the speech. Let your audience know you care deeply about the subject. You're probably thinking right now about the boring, fact-laden speech you have to deliver next week. You know, it doesn't have to be boring. There are ways to make any speech come alive. You infuse the presentation with lively anecdotes or current event issues or corporate stories that add flavor to the facts.

Enthusiasm or high energy means that you look eager and your body moves easily and effortlessly. Your face radiates confidence. You look as if you are actually enjoying yourself—**having fun with your body parts!**

We guarantee that when you enjoy public speaking, the audience enjoys you. We've seen good people with good ideas fail in public speaking because their style was flat and uninspiring. Don't allow that to happen to you. *Enthusiasm is contagious.*

Of course, you hit the proverbial home run when you are natural, prepared, and enthusiastic. Go for all three.

Let's Look at Some Recent Presidents...

Let's take a look at three recent American Presidents to see how they rate on our scale of being natural, prepared, enthusiastic.

Let's start with President Ronald Reagan. Was he natural when he spoke? Most people agree that he was. Was he enthusiastic? Yes. He seemed to like the role of President of the United States. Was Reagan prepared? Not always. Sometimes he was caught without the right information at his press conferences. Sometimes he seemed ill prepared and he said things he later had to recant. However, you recall that Mr. Reagan was known as the *Great Communicator*. His acting ability and his many years spent making public appearances helped him achieve that distinction.

How about President George Bush? Did Mr. Bush appear natural in his public appearances? Our observation was that the only time he seemed totally at ease and natural was when he was being interviewed at his vacation home in Kennebunkport, Maine. Was he prepared? Yes. He took great pains to show everyone that he had done his homework on various issues. But, was he enthusiastic? We don't think so. Of course, we're only talking about his image as a public speaker. For example, do you recall his televised debates with then candidate Bill Clinton? At one point the camera caught Bush checking his watch as if to say, "How much longer will I have to endure this?" This minor action was noticed and cued the audience that Mr. Bush was certainly feeling less than enthusiastic on that night.

Finally, what is your reaction to President Bill Clinton as a speaker? Was he natural? Seemed to be. Do you remember his Town Meetings during the campaigns? He talked directly to people in the audience about issues on their minds. He seemed to enjoy audience participation. Was Mr. Clinton prepared? He seemed to have an excellent grasp of the facts in every situation he encountered. And was he enthusiastic? One of Mr. Clinton's greatest assets as a speaker was his enthusiasm. He enjoyed every opportunity to speak and share ideas with audiences. He even handled himself gracefully in the State of the Union speech when he was under the pressure of the impeachment proceedings.

Remember these are not political opinions. We simply want you to be aware of what makes speakers good and what gets in their way. Make your own decision to be natural, prepared, and enthusiastic. Speaking in public will become a joy for you. And from now on, you'll begin to pay attention in new ways to every presentation you hear. You'll ask yourself, is this speaker natural, prepared and enthusiastic? You'll find it's really a lot of fun when you know what to look for in a speaker.

5.3 See Yourself Speaking: The Art of Visualization

You're now ready to move on to another great tool to help you become the speaker of your dreams: **Visualization.**

One way to make the speaking experience fun and easy is to use the visualization method to see, in your mind's eye, yourself standing there making a terrific speech.

According to Dr. Harry Emerson Fosdick, your visualization can lead to victory or defeat. He says, "Hold a picture of yourself long and steadily enough in your mind's eye and you will be drawn toward it...great living starts with a picture, held in your imagination, of what you would like to do or be."

Athletes have known about visualization techniques for some time. They're taught to actually see themselves achieving their goals. The most famous example of this may be Babe Ruth. Ruth must have been a master visualizer because in the fifth inning of the third game of the 1932 World Series against the Chicago Cubs, he took two straight strikes and pointed his finger at the most distant point in the outfield and slammed a homerun directly at that spot. He obviously saw the home run in his mind's eye before he came up to bat.

Arnold Palmer says that he "sees" where every golf shot will land before he drives or putts. Most athletes who participate in the Olympics say they see themselves in the heat of the competition as they train months or years ahead of the actual event.

The art of visualization is fairly simple. If you can actually see yourself doing something, the chances of doing it are greater than if you can't. This is great news for public speaking. We know for sure that most people see themselves feeling nervous and ill at ease when they get up to speak in front of an audience. They see their hands shaking, feel the heart palpitations, look out at that sea of faces and know the speech will be a disaster. And guess what? The speech fulfills that visualization.

How can we turn that scary scenario around? The first step is to do what you're doing right now—get the information you need to know about how to make a good speech. Learn it, practice it, know that you can be a great speaker, and finally SEE yourself up there feeling totally confident, enjoying the moment, relating to the audience, speaking with proper volume and cadence, and delivering a great speech. At the end of your speech, hear the applause and see the standing ovation, if that's what you want to happen. If you can visualize and see yourself in the picture you create, you are well on your way to giving a great speech.

Visualization can be a great tool to help you psyche yourself up for the big day. You might want to try the technique several times before the actual day of the speech. To visualize, relax and see yourself making the presentation and loving every minute of it. If thoughts of panic or fear enter your mind, simply say NO, and return to the mental picture of yourself enjoying your speech. Every time a negative image surfaces, cancel it out and replace it with a positive image.

Be willing to experiment with this technique. We know you'll be happy with the results. The next question to consider is how to handle your introductions.

5.4 Step Up With PEP: Fabulous Introductions

The PEP Formula for Introductions

Who will introduce you? Are you expected to introduce yourself? In either case, you need to prepare information about yourself before the day of the speech or presentation.

The introduction is an important preamble to your presentation. You want the audience to hear why you've been selected to speak. Incidentally, during the introduction you have a role to play, too. It is your responsibility to look directly at the person making the introduction and react to the words he or she is saying. Have you ever seen a person being introduced who is frantically leafing through notes and trying to get some last minute courage? Or have you seen the person looking all over the room but not at the person speaking? This is not only distracting, it's rude. Look at and react to the person giving the introduction.

The strange part of the introduction is this—most of the people in the audience will be looking at you, rather than the person introducing you. People want to get a quick overall impression of you, the speaker. The point is that your speech actually begins the moment the introducer mentions your name. This is no time to be distracted.

You'll need to provide the client or host with a one-page bio, which we call the **PEP formula**—**P** stands for your professional background. **E** for your education and expertise, and the final **P** is for personal and anecdotal information about you.

Let's take a look at the PEP formula:

1. **Professional Background**
   This is a brief description of your current job or career. It is essentially a quick overview of your history as it pertains to your overall credibility. For example, in this step you would mention

where you work, your job title and a comment or two about your current responsibilities. You might mention one or two major accomplishments you've achieved so far in your career.

2. **Expertise**

   You want to highlight one or two reasons why you have been chosen to give this particular speech or presentation. For example, if your speech is on computer technology, you'd want the audience to know you have spoken on this topic to several other groups or organizations. You'd also want this audience to know that you have won the Computer Specialist of the Year Award from your local chapter of computer wizards. If you've written books or if you've published articles on this or related subjects, you want to be sure the audience knows this. It's important for the introducer to mention your accomplishments. The person introducing you is in a position to paint a wonderful picture of you. The audience is getting ready to hear from an expert—You!

3. **Personal Anecdotes**

   You want the audience to know something personal about you before you go on. People love to know something private and personal about speakers. For example, the audience might like to know you are training for the Boston Marathon or that you are an active member of a local chorus. There are many personal stories to choose from. We talked about using anecdotes in your speech. Here's a chance to use one as part of your introduction. It will help to relax the presenter, the audience and you, too.

The personal anecdote does not have to fit into the subject of the speech. You might want your audience to know that you are the youngest of a clan of twelve brothers and sisters, and growing up in a large family made you aware of the power of teamwork and sharing. Even though your subject might not be specifically about team building, this is a good insight into the way you see life.

The most important thing about the PEP formula is that it makes the introduction easier for the person introducing you. The words should be simple and direct. The introduction should be very short (remember the introducer is usually not a public speaker so you want to make the PEP formula as easy to say as possible). Plan to send your introduction well ahead of the speaking date so the introducer can familiarize him or herself with it, but don't count on this to happen. Most people never look at the material until minutes before the speech. Another idea is to bring an extra copy with you. You know how easy it is to misplace a piece of paper and you want to make sure your introduction is as smooth as it can be.

Self-Introductions

Sometimes no one has been designated to introduce you. What do you do in these situations? It's important to establish yourself as someone who has the credentials to speak to this audience, but you may feel awkward about "tooting your own horn." Don't! You never get that second chance to make a good impression, so you're going to have to let go of any embarrassment and give yourself a solid introduction. Here are some tips for introducing yourself:

- **Start** by thanking the host or host organization.
- **Smile**. Pause and smile for a couple of seconds before you continue.
- **Give** the title and a quick overview of your topic.
- **Tell** why you're uniquely qualified to give this presentation.
- **Share** an anecdote about yourself or about your relationship to this audience.
- **Pause** as soon as you've finished your introduction.
- **Begin** the actual speech or presentation with your opening "grabber."

Whether you introduce yourself or someone else does it for you, it's important to get your speech or presentation off to a good start with **PEP**.

Work It Out

Take a few minutes to create your own PEP file. Once you've completed it, all you need to do is keep a copy on file and use it each time you speak. Obviously you'll want to update the information from time to time and to fit a particular speaking engagement.

MY PEP FILE:

1. **Professional Background**
2. **Expertise**
3. **Personal Anecdotes**

This is just one more step you are taking to become a speaking pro and to use all those precious body parts. Next we're going to take a look at what to eat to ensure that you have the right amount of energy for your speeches.

5.5 Sink Your Teeth Into This: Eating Right For High Energy

What you eat before you speak can and will make a difference. Many people choose to skip the meal just before the presentation because they say they're too nervous to eat anything. This is not a wise choice. You need proper nourishment to help you unleash the enormous amount of energy you need every time you speak in public.

To Get Ready For Your Morning Speech

Dr. Judith Wurtman, in her book **Managing Your Mind & Mood Through Food**, recommends that, for a morning speech, it's wise to eat *two* hours before the presentation so you'll be ready for the demands of the speech and the audience. She says:

> *"A good performance breakfast must be substantial enough to satisfy hunger after your seven-or eight-hour overnight fast, yet light enough and low enough in fat for quick, easy digestion."*

Plan to have juice, an egg, toast and coffee or tea for breakfast. Or you might try some oatmeal instead of the egg. When you arrive for the speech, don't be tempted to have a croissant, donut or sweet roll because this will offset the good you've done with the right breakfast.

To Get Ready For Your Afternoon Speech

Plan to eat less for lunch than you normally do. Your selections should be low on calories, fats and carbohydrates.

Sample meal: Chef salad with chicken, no salad dressing, whole grain roll and coffee or tea.

To Get Ready for Your After Dinner Speech

Skip hors d'oeuvres. Eat protein before carbohydrates. Eat about 1/3 of each portion you're served. Have coffee or tea if that is your normal preference.

Sample meal: Chicken, potato or rice (after eating some of the chicken), vegetable, coffee or tea.

How About a Drink to Soothe the Nerves?

Never drink alcohol before making a speech or presentation. Even one drink can change your mental acuity to the extent that your ability to relate to the moment and to the audience will be negatively affected. Dr. Wurtman says:

> *"Drink little or no alcohol the day of your performance; drink no alcohol in the three hours prior to your presentation."*

Some people think that a drink will help them relax, make them more comfortable with the audience, and less scared. This is what we call *excuse thinking*. When you're looking for any kind of a crutch to help you make a better speech, you haven't gotten yourself totally prepared—**and you know it**. Having a drink or two will not help you out in this situation and may hurt you and your reputation if anyone in the audience thinks you've resorted to drinking to find your courage.

The Best Combination

Whether you eat at home or at the site, eat *protein before carbohydrates* to keep your energy high. For example, at lunch eat the chicken or fish before you dig into the rest of the meal.

You're Ready

You've eaten right and you've decided to control those butterflies. You are ready to speak.

Step 6

Make a Great Speech

> *"Every artist was once an amateur."*
>
> —Ralph Waldo Emerson

Step 6 Make a Great Speech

"Think like a wise man but communicate in the language of the people."
—William Butler Yeats

6.1 Open Wide: Let the Speech Begin

Now we're going to talk about the speech itself. After you've done all the preparatory work, the Ideamapping, editing, and rehearsing, the day of the speech arrives. It's time to use all you've learned. It's time to share the ideas you've so carefully crafted.

We've been spending a lot of time on the thought process; now we're ready to begin the communication process. This next step is the one you've been preparing for. Let's go!

Confidence Builders

Every speaker must exude terrific **confidence**. How can you be sure you have all the confidence you need to make great presentations? First learn what successful speakers do—what tends to work for them. There's no need to reinvent the wheel. All good speeches have certain common characteristics. Find out what has worked for others and then add that information to your own personal toolbox, but make it your own. You cannot be a successful carbon copy of another speaker. You know it doesn't work.

Great Communicators

John F. Kennedy

Think about some of the great speakers we've heard or read about. We can still hear the words of President John F. Kennedy at his inaugural speech—*"Ask not what your country can do for you. Ask what you can do for your country."*

Martin Luther King Jr.

"I have a dream that my four little children will one day live in a nation where they will not be judged by the color of their skin, but by the content of their character...I have a dream today."

Eleanor Roosevelt

Eleanor Roosevelt was a shy young girl who was terrified at the thought of speaking in public. But with the passing years she grew in confidence and self esteem. She once said, "No one can make you feel inferior unless you agree with it."

Winston Churchill

"Let us brace ourselves to our duties, and so bear ourselves, that if the British Empire and its Commonwealth last for a thousand years, men will say *'This was our finest hour.'*"

Demosthenes (384-322 BC) The Greatest Athenian Orator

Demosthenes, the Athenian orator, is probably the greatest role model for anyone who has ever been accused of mumbling or speaking too softly. Many potentially spectacular speakers never make it to the podium because someone has made fun of a speech pattern such as mumbling. This old message seems to stay in the subconscious mind, and every time there is an occasion to speak, the mumbling returns.

Demosthenes was ridiculed by the other Athenian orators because he couldn't pronounce his Rs. However, he was determined to not only overcome his speech impediment, but to become the greatest orator in Athens.

To achieve his goal, he began to study the best orators of Greece. He rehearsed his speeches every day at the seashore, into the wind, making his voice stronger and stronger. To eliminate his stammer, he practiced every speech with his mouth stuffed with pebbles. When he was finally ready, he began to speak in public. Audiences were thrilled with his ability. Today, Demosthenes is known throughout the world as the greatest Athenian orator.

We might not recommend putting pebbles in your mouth as an exercise, but we do suggest that you study great speakers. What is it about them that makes them so effective? What do they have in common? Something to think about, isn't it?

Work It Out

Make a list of Great Communicators you have seen or heard. They can be public figures like Walter Cronkite, Ronald Reagan, Martin Luther King, Anthony Robbins, Oprah Winfrey, or people you know in your own family or at work. Next to the list of names select a word or two that describes the attribute you like about that communicator.

Great Communicators

NAME	ATTRIBUTE
1. Oprah Winfrey	Down to earth and real
2.	
3.	
4.	
5.	

Remember our advice—*Be yourself, and be your **best** self*. Learn from the experts and then develop your own style. There is no one right way to speak. That's one of the things that makes public speaking such a joy.

6.2 A Professional Approach

Stay on Time

One important hallmark of a good speaker is the ability to stay on time. Part of the mystique a speaker has to share is that he or she is speaking from the heart, and yet *totally* conscious of time. Audiences love to hear people speak extemporaneously, as if the thoughts are brand new and the words have never been spoken before.

While everyone knows that's just not possible, the trick is to sound as if you're actually thinking on your feet. One of the clearest signs of the practiced speaker is the ability to track time. If you've been given twenty minutes to speak, you should be on your closing statement at 19 minutes 40 seconds. Going over your allotted time, even by a few seconds, is the mark of an amateur.

Have you ever heard a speaker drone on well past his or her allotted time? We all have. Here's what happens—the speaker begins to lose audience attention rather quickly. Audiences seem to have built in time clocks, and when the speaker begins to abuse time it's a clear signal that he or she does not respect the audience.

Another down side of going over on time is the impact this has on the overall schedule. If each speaker exceeds the time limit by ten minutes, this can play havoc with the last speaker or the host speaker. It can even have a negative impact on the next speaker, because the long-winded speaker may put the audience into a negative frame of mind. That's not fair to the next speaker, is it? Even great speakers—the ones who mesmerize audiences—have to honor time commitments.

How do you manage to stay on time? The only way we know is to rehearse and rehearse until you get a feeling for how much time it takes for the opening, the body of the speech, and the closing. A word of caution here: We do not mean to imply that you should ever memorize your speech. No! We suggest that you rehearse ideas and the flow so much that you can look at your watch at any given time and know that you have to go for the close in so many minutes or seconds. Finishing on time has its own rewards. You'll be recognized as a complete professional. What is that worth?

Control Your Butterflies

Although we talked about FEAR at the beginning of the book, it's important to revisit it here, now that you're actually ready to get up and speak. What causes the butterflies we hear about? Who are these creatures that knot up our stomachs and sweat up our hands? The butterflies are actually friends called upon by the human body to protect it from danger. We are programmed to respond quickly to all perceived dangers. The body automatically releases adrenaline in sufficient amounts to help us handle any situation.

Have you ever been driving down a highway, relaxed and listening to some music, when suddenly a car swerves out of control ahead of you? What happens instantaneously? Your adrenaline pushes in and you react. Without this magnificent feature, life would be impossible.

When it comes to public speaking, the same thing happens as we step onto the stage to speak. There is danger there, although admittedly not of the same caliber as the potential auto accident. The danger in public speaking is more subtle. You can feel that you'll be attacked by the audience...maybe they won't accept you or your speech, your ideas, your credentials, your look, your clothes or any number of other things.

Some, or all of these, fears flood your body the minute you stand up to speak. Your body says, "Hurry, get the adrenaline," and the adrenaline appears. For most people, the adrenaline pump slows down almost immediately and returns the speaker to homeostasis, or neutral. But for some, the adrenaline continues to pump and pump and that's when the butterflies take over.

6.3 Five Quick Ways to Calm Your Body

1. **Before you go on the stage take three deep breaths**. Don't take in fat gulps of air, but slow, deep breaths through the nose, filling the lungs. Then exhale through the mouth. Repeat three times. You'll feel relaxed and energized. This is the mood you want for the speech. You can do this right before you get up to speak. Since the breathing is slow, no one will be able to see you doing it, yet this exercise will put your body in its ideal physical mode as you begin your presentation.

2. **Change your mind about the experience.** Know that you're going to be calm up there and the speech will be just as you planned it. Just knowing you're going to do well is often all you need to control the butterflies.

3. **Prior to getting up to speak, spend a little time with members of the audience.** We recommend arriving early enough to scope out the room, check the audio-visual equipment and to meet the people in a relaxed, friendly environment. Small talk is great talk for calming nerves. Of course, this is not always possible, so when you know you'll be unable to arrive early and "hang out" with people, try to learn as much as you can about individuals prior to the meeting so you do not feel as if you're the only stranger in the room.

4. **Know that you know your material.** There is nothing quite like solid preparation to help control butterflies. If you have spent the right amount of time getting ready, remind yourself of this fact just before you go on. It's good to recognize that you've done your homework and you're as ready as you need to be.

5. **Know that audiences want you to succeed.** Most audiences respect and admire speakers who are controlled and relaxed. If the speaker looks as if he or she is having a good time with the material, the audience relaxes and goes with the flow. It's when the speaker allows nervousness to control the environment that audiences feel the stress and begin to feel uncomfortable themselves. Most speakers who fail have, usually unwittingly, made the audience share their nervousness and audiences don't like the feeling any more than a speaker does.

6.4 Audiences Want The Best

When it comes right down to it, it's the audience that really counts, isn't it? Without the feedback from an audience, we simply don't know how well (or not so well) we're doing. Each audience has a personality of its own and that's something speakers need to know.

There is no such thing as a "one size fits all" audience anymore than there is a "one size fits all" speaker. Each is unique for the time and place. At Confidence Builders, we've learned this lesson because we often do two separate presentations in a day and while the key idea outline is exactly the same, the presentation will be different because of the personality of each audience. And this is the way it should be.

This is one of the main reasons we teach people to be flexible and to go with the flow in every speaking situation. If you've memorized a speech and you find an audience not responding, you're stuck. If, on the other hand, you give an extemporaneous speech based on your key idea outline, you'll be ready to go along with whatever a particular audience needs. It's amazing how one audience will cooperate and laugh in all the *right* places and another audience refuses to even recognize any humor in your presentation. This is what makes public speaking so fascinating.

Audience Reaction

It's a strange thing about audiences. They can be kind and somewhat less than kind at different points during your speech. Most audiences want speakers to succeed and they'll give every ounce of attention they can muster. They'll start out very forgiving because they've been speakers a time or two in their lifetimes, and they know all about the butterflies.

Most audiences will give the speaker a few minutes to find his or her pace, to settle down. However, if the speaker hasn't calmed down within two to three minutes, the audience's reaction changes from empathy to annoyance. If the speaker continues to be shaky, the audience can actually become silently hostile. It's a fact that most people will not be audible in their feelings. They'll simply sit back and tune out. The negative energy the speaker receives actually exacerbates the problem because now the speaker knows the audience is lost. What happens next is not a pretty sight. Most speakers start to speed up and talk faster and faster just to get through the ordeal and, as they do, the mouth dries up and the voice starts to crack. It's a sad spectacle to observe. Have you ever seen it happen to a speaker? Has it ever happened to you? If so, you know precisely how it feels. Not good.

Be A Little Bit Better

Know that you must prepare. You have no alternative if you expect to be a successful speaker.

> *"It usually takes more than three weeks to prepare a good impromptu speech."*
> —Mark Twain

But here's something to consider—it is not necessary to be a super star speaker to be a *successful* speaker. You can get the audience's attention, admiration, and feedback just by being **a little bit better** than other speakers. This thought bears repeating—just be a little bit better and you will make a favorable impression on most audiences. Many speakers think they have to speak like a pro in order to measure up. No wonder people freeze. If you are natural, prepared, and enthusiastic, your audiences will respect you. **Respect is one of the most important ingredients in effective public speaking.** Without it, a speaker stands little chance of being heard. How do you earn that respect?

One of the smartest things you can do as a speaker is to care more about the audience than you care about yourself while you are up there speaking. This may sound difficult, given the idea that public speaking is so scary for most of us, it seems natural to worry about how we're doing, second by second. However, the best speakers are those who are able to put themselves on the other side of the fence and understand how the audience will feel and react. It's the audience's comfort and understanding you're seeking, not your own!

So many would-be speakers are so concerned about their own butterflies and their own security, they forget that a speech is for the people in the audience. We have found that the more speakers focus on self, the less they connect with the audience. This behavior doesn't make sense, yet *inexperienced speakers hardly ever worry about how the audience is doing.* It takes a great sense of presence to put your feelings and fears aside for the good of the audience, but it is this very presence that makes you stand out.

Dorothy's Story:

In the early 1980s I worked with the president of a large retail operation. He was used to giving many speeches and presentations during the course of a year. I heard him speak one time at an association meeting and I was surprised to find that this very successful man gave one of the most boring speeches I had ever heard. Eventually, he was referred to me for private speech coaching. I helped him liven up his presentations with some anecdotal material and he developed a faster pace.

He told me during our first session that he had always thought he was an excellent speaker. He said he had asked for feedback from his managers, and they always told him he did a great job. Obviously this man was insensitive to audience reaction or he would have known that something wasn't working. He was shocked to find out how boring he really was and he said, "If only someone had told me sooner." Top executives are often the last to know how good or bad they are because the people who report to them are afraid to be honest. Get honest feedback.

6.5 Put Your Mind At Ease

Select A Key Target

As you stand there, ready to speak, look out at your audience in total silence. You display your poise and presence when you take a little time (we recommend about five to seven seconds) before saying your first words. As you glance around the room, select a friendly looking face as far in the back of the room as possible. This person will become your *focal point*. You're going to say your whole opening statement directly to him or her.

Look into that person's eyes as you complete your entire opening statement. Remember, we said that the opening should be short and a "grabber." Once you've completed that short phase of the speech, you must begin to move your eyes around to other people. We'll show you how to do just that in the next section.

Selecting a key target helps you in two ways. You focus all of your attention on that one person, but everyone else hears you, and because the person is all the way in the back of the room, you are forced to speak up and speak more forcefully. When you use this technique, you'll create energy for yourself and for your audience.

Select a key target in the back of the room and deliver your opening to that real person.

Smiling Faces

A friendly face will do more to calm you down than almost anything else. Seeing someone who appears nice helps you get over your initial jitters. We've known some speakers who try to find the harshest looking face in the room. They think if they can win that person over, they'll win with everyone. Why put yourself in this kind of a position? We always recommend finding your personal comfort zone and working within it. Friendly faces help.

How Does the Audience Respond To You?

How can you gauge audience response during your speech? Is it possible to know what's going on in an audience as you are actually speaking? Yes. You know that as a member of an audience yourself many times, you are given to scratching, yawning, looking around, talking, reading, and a lot of other behaviors that indicate you are not always 100 percent with the speaker. As we mentioned earlier, our studies have shown that most people can only concentrate for short spurts of time—on average about 20 percent of the total time you're speaking. Wow! That's not much, is it? What this means is that as a speaker, you have a huge responsibility to pull people back into your train of thought when they slip away. How do you do this?

Maintaining Audience Interest

1. **Closely Watch Audience Behavior.** Pay close attention to what's going on in general. Does the audience seem attentive or bored? Are people looking at you as you speak, or are they reading or chatting with a neighbor? Do you notice any yawning or eyes closing or are they returning your eye contact? Is there laughter from time to time or is there little or no audience reaction?

You must be aware of audience dynamics. It's up to you and you alone to change the atmosphere if you are not satisfied with how the audience is responding to you. For example, if you notice that people are beginning to nod off a bit, you'll need to do or say something dramatic to refocus their attention. Or you might need to check the heat or lack of air circulation in the room. Often, it's the stuffiness in a room that creates a lot of nodding and closed eyes. It will be up to you to check on such things and change them if possible. If this is not possible, you might want to consider asking people to stand up and stretch. Physical movement can help. It also shows the audience that you are very much in control of the situation and aware of their discomfort.

2. **Speak Louder or Softer**. People tend to drift away during a speech that is given in a monotone voice. You have to raise or lower your voice from time to time to keep the attention of the audience. Some speakers actually shout at some point in the speech, and whisper at another time. It's this modulation that makes a speaker interesting. You may have to practice this speaking style since many new speakers are hesitant to try new methods. During your rehearsal time, try *shouting* out a very dramatic or important point. Then try *whispering* something that you want the audience to perceive as personally revealing. When you actually try these ideas in front of a live audience, you'll be amazed at the response you'll get.

3. **Ask Questions, If Appropriate.** If your speech is structured to encourage audience participation, plan to ask simple questions when you notice the audience is beginning to drift. This is a great way to get people back on track. For example, you can suddenly ask them to write down two thoughts and then ask someone for a quick answer. People love to be involved.

4. **Do Not Confront.** It is not a good idea to confront someone who is simply not paying attention. To do so can be embarrassing to the person in the audience and can backfire on you. There are a couple of things you can do. The best one is to use really strong eye contact on someone who is not looking at you. It's amazing how powerful eye contact is. The person feels your strong eye contact and his or her eyes often automatically come back to you. Nothing is said, but you've made your point. Another thing

you can do is speak in general terms, *"I know it's tough to stay awake after a big lunch. We'll be taking a break soon."* That's a general statement, so no one will take offense at it.

5. **Let Them Know You Are Totally Present.** It is just as important to be present *emotionally* as well as physically. That is, it's critical that *you* are not looking around or looking at your watch, or in any way seeming nervous or eager to get out of the room. Many speakers race through the presentation, and it seems that they would rather be any place other than in that room at that time.

    One way to ensure that you're meeting an audience's needs is to ask for questions after your formal remarks. We've seen remarkable connections made during the q & a sessions that might have been lost if the speaker hadn't been willing to be open and vulnerable because you never know what an audience is thinking until you open the floor to questions. (More about handling questions and answers coming up later.)

6.6 Your Eyes: A Powerful Body Part

Why are the eyes so important? It is through the eyes of others that we learn how we're doing when we speak. Many speakers refuse to look at people at all when they speak, and that's a major mistake. The old saying *"The eyes are the mirror of the soul"* takes on new meaning when applied to public speaking. It is with eye contact that you let people know you are really present, right there, not wishing to be anywhere else.

How many of us took the old Speech 101 class in which the professor gave us this advice: *"To avoid nervousness, pick a spot on the back of the wall and speak to it."* What does that mean? Imagine how it would look if a speaker stood there, behind the lectern, staring at some smudge on the back wall while issuing words of wisdom for two or three minutes. How do you think you'd feel as a member of the audience? Before long you'd be turning around trying to see who's in the back of the room getting all that attention. The better way is to use eye contact in the way we're going to recommend.

First, understand this idea: **No Eyes, No Talk.**

This means that you should not be talking **at all** if your eyes are not locked into someone else's eyes. What about when you're looking at notes or leafing through overhead transparencies? When you pause to look up information or to get your bearings, you must **stop talking**. NO EYES, NO TALK! It only takes a second or two to find your place or to put up a new transparency. As soon as you are ready to begin again, find a new pair of eyes and start talking.

One of the great side effect benefits of this rule is elimination of those uninvited "ums" and "uhs" that seem to vie for center stage when you're speaking. We've observed over and over again that these non-words tend to pop out when you are looking up at the ceiling, off to the side or down on the floor. To noticeably reduce the number of "ums" in a presentation, pause briefly as you make the transition from one idea to another. It's natural to look up, down, or sideways during this transition time. Just don't talk. When you're ready, return to a pair of eyes and start speaking again.

What will happen? You'll find that people will respond more favorably to you because they will feel they are part of the presentation. When you look into people's eyes you're giving off a clear message, *"I'm not afraid of anyone in this room, and I'm willing to share my ideas with all."* That's one powerful message.

Four Seconds

How do you make sure you're using eye contact effectively? There have been many studies done on the appropriate amount of time to spend with each person. When you are making a presentation, we've found that the **Four-Second Eye Contact** rule seems to work best because four seconds is neither too long nor too short an amount of time to make a connection with someone in the audience.

We've observed that **four seconds** is just about right to get the person to realize that you are looking at him or her and to get an almost imperceptible nod. If the eye contact time is too short (1-3 seconds) it appears that you're not looking at anyone at all, or that you're nervous, and if it's too long (6 seconds or more), you appear to be confrontational.

Anyone who's been to church or synagogue knows the power of eye contact. Sometimes it seems the minister, priest or rabbi is talking directly to you. You know the feeling—he or she is looking right at me. This message is for me! Have you ever been to a concert and felt that the singer was singing directly to you (even though there were thousands of people there)? You want to achieve the same kind of result. The more people feel they are part of what's happening, the more attention they'll pay to you and your ideas. It happens through the power of eye contact.

The best advice we can give you to master eye contact is to try it. See how people respond when you're sharing eye contact. At the beginning, you'll probably feel a little awkward, as if you're staring. Some people have to count it out (silently, of course) one thousand one, one thousand two, one thousand three, one thousand four. That's four seconds. Try it on friends and try to go longer or shorter to gauge the reaction. We think you'll find, as we did, that four seconds works best.

Be careful. We don't want you to be too mechanical about this eye contact business. Don't start at the left-hand side of the room and go from person to person as if you're an automaton. Eye contact should be shared around the room randomly and automatically.

We know that every audience gives off lots of energy. Tap into the energy in the room. For example, you might notice that someone in the back row seems particularly interested in a certain point you're making—keep your eyes sharply focused on that person for four seconds. Next you might notice that a person sitting on the aisle in the middle of the room seems to be drifting—focus on her and chances are good you'll regain her attention. And on and on throughout your speech.

The whole idea behind good eye contact is *sharing*. You want to be able to share ideas with everyone and one of the best ways to accomplish it is through eye contact. It's amazing how much information is transferred from eye to eye.

Notice the next time you're in an audience how the speaker uses or *abuses* eye contact. You'll be amazed at the difference good eye contact makes and how uninspired you feel when you're trying to listen to a person who does not pay attention with his or her eyes. And how involved you feel when someone looks at you from time to time.

Here's How to Master the Eye Contact Concept

1. **Never speak to dead air**. Look into someone's eyes whenever words are coming out of your mouth. (No eyes, No talk.)

2. **Hold eye contact for four seconds**. Count one thousand one, one thousand two, one thousand three, one thousand four (not out loud).

3. **Move on to another pair of eyes**. This transition takes virtually no time at all. During the move from one person to another, do not speak. If you do, it will probably be an "uh" or an "um" and you don't want those non-words in your speech. If you want to control this tendency, try to pause for a second or two as you ponder your next thought and then move to a new pair of eyes. Try it. It's a powerful sign of speaker presence.

4. **Repeat the 4-second process again and again** throughout the speech, making sure to reach all parts of the room at some point in the presentation.

5. **When referring to notes, glance quickly at the notes without speaking**. When you are ready, find a pair of eyes and continue the presentation.

6. **During pauses, look around the room to assess current audience involvement.** Look toward the high-energy spots and force yourself to look at the low energy or dead spots from time to time to see if you can recapture someone who's wandered off mentally.

7. **Do not have eye contact with only one or two people** and leave the rest of the audience out. The ones who feel left out will likely rate your presentation as mediocre at best, and they might not even know why. Eye contact creates connections and that's what you're trying to achieve every time you speak.

8. **Enjoy the process of actually seeing people as you speak.** It's a way to make a connection. We know that sometimes you're subjected to stage lighting and you really can't see anyone in the audience. On those occasions, look toward various sections of the auditorium from time to time. Try, whenever possible to have the stage lit so you can actually see people in the audience.

The Payoff

The most important benefit from using eye contact is that it makes the audience feel important. They know you are talking directly to them and with them, not *at* them. So many people who get up to speak are so concerned with themselves and how they are performing, they forget to concentrate on the needs of the audience. And every audience can sense this misplaced focus. They don't like it and they shouldn't like it. Remember that **your audience is more important than you are**. People who understand this philosophy are on the road to becoming great speakers.

Work It Out

The Eyes Have It

For this exercise, it's best to ask a friend to work with you as your coach. Gather a small group of people you know and trust. Tell them you're practicing a new story telling technique. Then tell a favorite anecdote or a joke. Ask one friend to watch your eyes to make sure you're spending **four seconds of eye contact** with each person in the group. Have your coach silently count out *one thousand one, one thousand two, one thousand three, one thousand four* and then with a nod or a hand signal, motion you on to the next person.

Take about two minutes to tell your story. When you've finished, ask the people in the group how they felt as you were telling the story. You should get answers like, *"I felt you were talking directly to me."* or *"I was really involved with the story."* These answers indicate that you were reaching the people with both your story and your eyes. If you don't get this kind of response, chances are good your eye contact was limited.

As soon as possible after the experience, talk with your designated coach to get feedback on how your eye contact was working. If it was too quick, one to two seconds, which is usually the case for beginners, practice staying with it a bit longer. The old countdown method works best...*one thousand one, etc.* "Practice makes perfect" is exactly the idea you need when it comes to eye contact. Try the four-second method and you'll be thrilled with the results you get.

Wandering Eyes

What happens when you use eye contact but some people in the audience don't look back? Sometimes an audience member looks out the window, glances at the door, reads a newspaper, or in other ways shows he or she is not paying attention. You have to realize that some people are unaware of the value of eye contact, and some people simply don't like it. It makes them feel uncomfortable or uneasy. The key idea is to use eye contact with as many people as possible during your talk, and don't worry if someone refuses to play. Just go on to the next pair of eyes.

6.7 Where Are Your Hands Anyway?

One of the questions that often comes up at our presentation skills seminars is this one. *"What do I do with my hands?"* Good question. We often talk about the position most people use when they're speaking—hands clasped tightly in front of them, which in our profession is called the *fig leaf* position. When someone clasps hands behind the back, it's called the *reverse fig leaf*.

When your hands are in either fig leaf or reverse fig leaf position, you're actually holding your energy *in* rather than letting it *out*. No wonder so many people feel nervous when they speak. Without realizing it, we sometimes actually create our own tension just by the way we use our body parts.

Fig Leaf   Reverse Fig Leaf

The recommended hand position is simply to have your hands resting at your sides when they are not in use. Now, your hands will work *naturally* to reflect the amount of energy and enthusiasm you have. Some people use their hands a lot in their everyday speech mannerisms. Others are quieter, keeping hand gestures to a minimum. Whatever is normal for you in your everyday speaking pattern should be used when you're on the platform.

Some professional speech coaches recommend that you actually plan your hand gestures along with the words of your speech. We don't see how this can work effectively because your hands are merely extensions of your thought process, and if you leave your hands alone, they will do exactly what they're supposed to do. Of course, if you find yourself going into the fig leaf position, you do have to think about changing that behavior. Simply unlock your hands, drop them to your sides and begin all over again.

The idea is, don't worry about your hands. Let them help you emphasize your ideas and they will. Worry about gestures and your hands will look like separate appendages and you may find them out of sync with your words. That looks peculiar to the audience and you lose credibility.

Imagine trying to program your hands to show the number 5 during your speech. If you're reading your speech (please don't) and you've written down hand gestures to use, here's how it will work: You are reading along and you come to "We are announcing our brand new 5 Point Marketing plan." This is when you see you're supposed to insert a hand gesture holding up five fingers. You pause for one second while you read the little hand gesture instruction to yourself, and that is one second too long. Your gesture is simply too late to go with your words. Your hand is out of sync with your words and you look foolish. It's like telling a joke and missing the precise timing of the punch line. More embarrassing than funny.

Work It Out

Here's a little exercise you can try. Get a group of 3-6 people together. Ask everyone to stand with hands at their sides at the speaker ready position. Then you say, "Show me what something huge looks like." Watch the gesture. Then say, "Show me something really small." And, "Show me something as big as the world." You'll find that everyone knows how to use his or hands perfectly. The actual gestures may vary slightly, but the point is made that the hands work automatically. They do not have to be programmed or scripted.

Pockets or Not?

What about keeping your hands in your pockets? That's a very casual look and a lot of speakers think being casual is a form of showing control. We think having your hand in your pocket is a little too casual especially as you begin the speech or talk. At the beginning, you want your audience to sit up and take notice of you as a complete professional. That means you want to use every opportunity at your disposal to make that great first impression. As you get deeper into the talk, you might feel comfortable with your hands in your pockets for a *very short period of time,* particularly if you're trying to help the audience relax. However, if you keep your hands in your pockets for any longer period of time, your energy will certainly begin to diminish and you don't want that to happen.

Hands on Hips

We've noticed that a lot of people in our seminars like to stand and talk with their hands on their hips. It looks like a military style and we recommend you avoid this position when making a presentation because, once again, with hands on hips, you are closing off some potentially good hand gestures that can actually help you drive home points. The audience may actually misinterpret your message if you keep your hands on your hips too long. They could read the gesture as aggressive when that is not what you intended.

The next time you hear a speaker, pay close attention to his or her hands. We'll bet that most of the speakers you'll see will be locked in that fig leaf position for the majority of the time. However, if you see a really great speaker, professional or not, the hands will be used effectively to carry the words.

Using your hands properly is really quite simple. Keep them in action and they'll serve you well. Keep them tied up in front of you or behind you, or keep one in your pocket and your energy level will automatically decrease. Since energy is the fire of the speech, you want to stoke that fire constantly. Your hands are great tools. Use them freely to help you punctuate ideas.

6.8 Posture & Pacing

Posture is important in speaking. We recommend that you stand up tall, but not stiff. Don't hunch up your shoulders or try to have military-style posture. You want to have a relaxed, but ready look. Feet planted firmly on the floor. Hands at your sides. Establish eye contact with someone in the audience. Pause before the opening. Stand tall as if to say you know exactly what you're doing—because you do.

It's amazing how important those first few seconds are in establishing a speaker's credibility. If you're fidgeting or pulling and pushing yourself, your clothes, your overheads, or your notes, you'll look ill prepared and the audience will have an "uh-oh" feeling. The "uh-oh" feeling means that the audience is afraid the speaker is going to be dull and boring. As speakers, we never want to give that impression because it's a hard one to shake once it's been established.

Dorothy's Story

I love to attend seminars and listen to other speakers. I always learn something. Recently, I attended a Financial Seminar. The first thing the instructor did was to forget to plug in the overhead projector. She scrambled to get it going, then she couldn't focus the projector. Next, her name was printed on the cover of the handout with a series of initials following her name, M.A., CFIC. Someone in the audience said, "What do the initials stand for?" She said the M.A. was Master of Arts and then she said, "The C stands for certified and the F for Financial. The I— Oh I can't remember exactly what these letters mean." She lost the audience from that moment on. With these two actions her credibility was gone! All of this took place within the first 30 seconds of her presentation and the next two hours were very uncomfortable for everyone in the audience.

Postures to Watch

Your posture is a dead giveaway that reveals either nervousness or control. Every audience can spot your comfort zone immediately. Our bodies tell the whole story and sometimes in subtle ways.

The Pacer

For example, did you ever see a *walk here, walk there, walk everywhere* speaker? We've seen this marathoner many times in our seminars. The posture is fine, it's the pacing back and forth and side to side that is the signal that this speaker is nervous.

You should move naturally. You never want to appear frozen in place. There is a fine line between sincere movement to make a point or to emphasize an idea and random pacing that drives audiences nuts.

When you are speaking to a large audience from the stage, and if you're not behind the lectern, you'll have to move back and forth across the stage to make sure the audiences on both sides of the auditorium can see you. Pace yourself. You do not need to move constantly. Spend a few minutes on the right side and then spend a couple of minutes in the middle of the stage and then move left. All of these moves should seem effortless and perfectly natural. Proper stage presence is really about connecting with the audience.

We know that audiences create energy and that energy is transmitted to the speaker. Good speakers pick up on that energy and move toward it. So, if you feel that the energy is coming from the right, your tendency is to move there. If it's coming from the back of the room, you move toward the front of the stage. Have you ever watched a motivational speaker like Les Brown, Anthony Robbins, or Zig Ziglar? They move a lot, but each move means something. Good speakers know how to move in time with audience reactions.

The Swayer

Another distracting habit is swaying from side to side. Have you ever watched a speaker sway from side to side and wonder if the person has fallen into some kind of a trance? Most often, the speaker is totally unaware that he or she is in the swaying mode. It's a constant moving from one foot to another. You've seen this in small children whose mommies ask them to sing a little song and they feel a bit nervous, so they sing and sway. It's cute when the kid is three, not so cute when the speaker is thirty-three.

The Rocker

Then there's the rocker. This is the speaker who rocks forward and then rocks back again and again throughout the entire presentation. This speaking behavior is a clear sign of nervousness and creates such a distraction that it's difficult to follow the speech.

Dead or Alive?

Finally there's the speaker who stands totally still as if moving a single muscle will make him or her forget the entire speech. We've all seen this type. The audience waits and watches to see if he or she will ever move. This eerie stillness becomes a distraction and the speaker's words and ideas are often lost. Unfortunately, people tend to be more interested in the speaker's discomfort than the message.

Habits

The best thing about posture is that it's easy to change bad habits. We've found that becoming aware of what you do is often all you'll need to begin to change the behavior

The best advice we can give is to relax when you're up there speaking. One way to do this is to take some deep breaths before you go on and to do some self talk about how much you're going to enjoy this speaking experience. And when you find yourself feeling stiff or swaying or rocking stop and take another deep breath.

A lot of what you're learning in this book is about what has worked for other speakers. We recommend that you begin today to watch other speakers carefully. See what works and what does not.

Use Your Camcorder to Check out Your Posture

Another recommendation is to videotape yourself at some point during the rehearsal phase so you can see how you actually look when you speak. A videotape doesn't lie and it doesn't try to make you feel better about yourself. See what you see and make appropriate changes. This is the time to be totally honest. If you find yourself boring, imagine what the audience will find!

If you do not have a camcorder available, ask someone to watch your rehearsal or the presentation itself and to give you honest feedback about everything, including your posture.

What Makes Audiences React?

Clothing

We're not going to spend much time on the subject of clothes except to point out that it's relatively easy to be appropriately dressed. The key word is *appropriate*. This is not at all about how much money you spend for clothes, but that it's important to dress for the occasion. If you're making a speech in most corporate boardrooms, you don't want to show up in Levis and tennis shoes, but if you're doing a presentation at a resort, it's probably all right to wear a jacket and slacks (for both men and women).

The idea is that you want to fit in. Our suggestion is that you always *go one step above* what the people in the audience are wearing. So, if your speech is in a city environment, you might want to wear a conservative suit or dress and quiet tie or scarf. If your speech is at a resort, and everyone is wearing Dockers and Tee shirts, you'll probably feel more comfortable wearing slacks and a coat (no tie or scarf) and then removing the jacket at some point if that seems appropriate.

7 Seconds to Decide

One of the strange things about being a human being is the way we look at and evaluate other human beings. Studies show that we are quick to decide...some experts in communications say we do it within *seven seconds*. That is, we look at someone and immediately process information about that person based on preconceived perceptions.

We go into our brain bank to pick out immediate similarities. The brain, in a sense, asks, "Does this person remind me of someone I know?" All of this sifting and sorting goes on within milliseconds. The brain's computer swiftly documents everything we *think we know* about this type of person and, in seconds, we've made a decision—right or wrong!

The same brain action happens every time someone gets up in front of an audience to speak. The brain asks, "Who's this?" And there it goes, making that seven second decision again. Since we all do it, at least there's a level playing field. I judge you, but you judge me. The important thing is to realize that this quick analysis is a human reaction. Be ready to be judged. That's why your mother always told you to put your best foot forward. (And wear clean underwear!)

6.9 Presence & Attitude

"The greatest discovery of my generation is that human beings can alter their lives by altering their states of mind."
—William James

Attitude, which is the great indicator of Presence, is the do or die element in public speaking. When you decide to become a good speaker, you become one. It's that simple. Since you're reading this book right now, chances are excellent that you're planning to become a super speaker. Oh, you might still be in the throes of fear and uncertainty at this moment. That's all right. What you're really saying to yourself is this: *"There must be some big secret to this public speaking."* And there is. In addition to *Exercising Your Body Parts*, the secret to good public speaking is ATTITUDE. Those who think they can speak in public can, and those who think they can't speak in public can't.

"If you think you can do a thing or think you can't do a thing, you're right."
—Henry Ford

When we think we cannot do something, we usually don't even try to do it; therefore, we leave a blank in our lives. We'll simply never know if we could have been successful. Of course, the real message in Ford's comment is to try new things. Adopt the attitude that you can be a good speaker. You can. Here are some tips.

Enjoy the Moment: Audiences know immediately if you are enjoying yourself when you are up there speaking. The audience seems to have a hidden radar detector that goes off and says, "Yes, this person is confident and secure up there." Or, the radar detector that says, "Uh, oh, trouble. This speaker is not having a good time with this presentation." As soon as the audience decides, one way or the other, the tone for the whole presentation is set. It is difficult, although not impossible, to change the effect once you've established it. The best advice we can give is to choose to enjoy the opportunity to share your ideas. How? Simply say these words to yourself before you go on:

"I'm going to enjoy every moment up there." Try it. You'll be surprised at how powerful this suggestion is to help you see the speaking situation in a new, different, and better way.

Be Present: Don't go to the "zone" so many speakers disappear into when they are in the spotlight. The zone is the time warp that makes present time disappear. We have often seen a speaker stand on stage, say the words, show the slides, and breathe a sigh of relief when his or her time on the platform is up, and never remember a thing about the experience. That speaker is zoning. You want to be there for yourself and for your audience. This means you are awake and aware of every single thing that is going on.

Smiling: Okay we've said this before but it bears repeating again and again. A genuine smile not only helps the audience relax and really listen to you, it helps to calm you down. We're not talking about forced or phony smiles. You know the audience picks up on any degree of phoniness, so don't do the artificial smile. It won't work. It is never a good idea to program a smile. Do smile automatically when the feeling comes over you. Smiling comes from within and when it happens naturally, people feel good and so do you. The point is to think about allowing yourself to relax enough to smile from time to time.

Breathing: Your words need air to ride on. Breathing properly will make a major difference in how your voice sounds. If you take shallow breaths, keeping the air in your upper throat, your voice will sound weak and higher than normal. Shallow quick breathing can also lead to lightheadedness and that's usually the first cause of nervousness. It's not a great idea to gulp in huge quantities of air either; however, you do need an even flow of air to be able to speak comfortably and avoid the mumbling that sometimes occurs when you are just about out of breath. Focus on breathing from the diaphragm. This means, for most of us, taking deeper breaths, but not gulping air. You can change the quality of your voice and its projection by doing some deep breathing exercises before you speak.

Pacing: When we talk about pacing, we're talking about your personal body language. How do you look up there during the entire presentation? Do you start off with high energy and then wind down to monotony? Or do you start off at a snail's pace and wind up running around like a cheetah? Pacing is a physical element that clearly shows your attitude when you speak. It is important to vary your pace physically as well as vocally. You do not want to stand in one position with no movement for the whole speech or presentation. Audiences get fidgety and bored with speakers who seem to be stuck. You don't want to be in constant motion either. Constant motion puts the audience on edge and distracts from the message you are trying to give. Our best advice is to think about what you are trying to convey in your speech or presentation and match your body movements and pacing to that. For example, if you're talking about the company's outstanding quarterly results, your pacing should reflect your excitement about the results. You'll probably be more animated than if you're talking about the business plan for the upcoming year. Be appropriate (and you know what is appropriate for you personally and for the occasion).

The One-Two Punch: It's important to emphasize, punctuate or *punch* certain words and phrases during the course of your presentation. To avoid monotony, you have to spend some time in the rehearsal phase defining the words or phrases you need to pay particular attention to. For example, you might want to raise your voice to show excitement, whisper for a sense of intimacy with the audience, speak in a rapid-fire way sometimes and then slow down considerably. Sometimes you might want to repeat a statement because it is so important. All of these vocal varieties can enhance your presentation. However, it's important to understand that these techniques will only work if they are natural. The audience will be completely on to what you are doing if your vocal variety seems too rehearsed and forced. They don't like to feel that a speaker is over-rehearsed. Remember, a speech is not a part in a play. It's important for you to rehearse and try out these vocalizations so they flow with both the extemporaneous thought and emotion you are trying to convey, without sounding staged. The audience should have the sense that your presentation is seamless. Never forced or artificial.

The Power of the PAUSE: Presence includes your ability to control the flow of information. One of the clearest indicators of a professional speaker is his or her ability to *pause* at appropriate points in the speech or presentation. Begin your speech with a 5-7 second pause. This pause lets the audience know you are poised and waiting for your perfect moment before you say the first word.

A sure mark of an amateur is the need to fill every second with words. Have you noticed speakers who seem to go on and on and never take a breath? As audience members, we become breathless ourselves. That kind of speaker is showing a lack of experience and poise. A speaker who is in control knows that carefully selected pauses punctuate meaning. For example, if I'm talking about a stressful situation and I say quickly, "I couldn't eat and I couldn't sleep," the feeling I'm trying to express might be lost on the audience. If I change the cadence slightly and say, " I couldn't eat." (Pause for a count of 2.) "I couldn't sleep." (Pause for a count of 3.) The pauses between the ideas create an interesting and dramatic tension the audience picks up. The words are the same; it's the pause that makes the difference.

Pauses allow audience members to catch up with and catch on to what the speaker is saying.

How do you know when to pause? As you go about the process of developing and rehearsing your speech, you'll begin to realize that there are definite places where a pause will work. You can actually place a *pause mark* in your key idea outline, so when you come to that place, you'll know to stop and take a breath. The audience will know you've made an important or a poignant point. Another time to pause is right after telling a story or a joke. Many speakers actually lose the moment by speaking too soon. If you've said something funny or heartwarming, stop and be silent long enough to allow the feeling to fill the room for a few seconds before you go on.

The final pause comes at the end of the speech itself. Before you go on to take questions, pause for a full five seconds. Or, if you do not plan to take questions, pause for 3-4 seconds as soon as you've delivered your closing remarks. There is no more important time to pause than at the close. You display great presence by holding your silence for those few seconds at the end of your speech. The novice does not do this. Instead, he or she almost runs away from the spotlight the second the last word is uttered. Pausing is a dramatic, yet simple way to show your audiences that you are a professional.

We believe all those body parts we love to talk about are the packaging around the **attitude** the speaker brings to the situation. If a person is willing to share ideas openly and freely and with conviction, the audience senses this immediately. Your attitude ultimately makes your presentation a failure or a success. Go for success!

6.10 At the Heart of the Matter: Question & Answer Techniques

Once you've finished your presentation, it's a great idea to ask for questions from the audience. What happens next is almost *magical*. You've finished the formal part of the presentation and now you're going to stand there and face the unknown. Be sure to allow yourself some time at the end of your presentation to pause and accept applause if that is appropriate. You don't want to hasten this moment. If you rush, you'll seem amateurish. Just stand quietly for a few seconds, smiling and maintaining eye contact with the audience, and then ask for questions.

You don't know what kinds of questions people might come up with, so you have to be prepared to be vulnerable. At this point, you can literally step out from behind the lectern if you've been using one, and face the audience with your full body. This is a definite signal that you're not afraid to handle any questions that might arise.

Plan to include a question & answer session as part of your speech. The payoff is tremendous. If you've had to present tough or difficult information or if the presentation is not terribly exciting, here's your chance to shine. In the question and answer period you'll be able to elaborate and expand on your ideas.

What a great opportunity! Take advantage of this. Don't be afraid that you won't be able to answer the questions. If you've used the prepping methods we've recommended in this book, you'll have much more information than you can use in the actual speech. This is the time to bring up all those extra facts you simply couldn't fit into the presentation itself.

Before the presentation, be sure to ask your host or program planner how much time will be allowed for the q & a session. Don't exceed that time limit (even though at times it will be tempting).

10 Techniques Related To Handling Questions

1. **Do not interrupt!** This is easier said than done. So often, the person asking the question will ramble on and on and you'll want to jump in and begin the answer because you sense you know

exactly where the question is going and you already have the answer. The problem in interrupting is two-fold: first it's simply rude, and second, you may not really hear the heart of the question. Recent studies show that people tend to get to the real kernel of the idea toward the end of their question rather than at the beginning. That's because some people know what they're thinking but find it hard to express themselves. You must give the questioner time to formulate the question.

There are three times when this rule does not apply: If the person is into grandstanding, i.e., making a speech of his or her own at your expense, you need to interrupt. It isn't fair to the audience for someone to try to take over your platform. Interrupt that person. Another legitimate time to interrupt is when the rambling is excessive, when you know the person is not getting to the point at all. Help that person with a summarizing question such as, *"So, you're asking me if X is related to Y, right?"* And immediately begin your answer—even if that's not really the exact question the person had in mind. The third time to interrupt is if you know the questioner is presenting a lie. For example, the questioner says, *"Isn't it true that your accounting practices are questionable and"* interrupt right then and say *"You know that's false. Let's get a real question."* You don't want the questioner to get away with that kind of outrageous comment. It isn't appropriate. Trying to answer such a question can only lead to speculation and gossip.

2. **Maintain eye contact** with the person asking the question throughout the entire question. It's important to maintain eye contact because it's a sign of respect. Have you ever seen a speaker looking at her notes the whole time a question is being asked? This is not only rude, it gives a clear signal that the answer is probably not coming from the speaker's own wisdom and experience, and that can be distracting to the audience. Incidentally, it's fine to refer to notes or perhaps a visual-aid reference that will help you to answer the question. It's a matter of timing. When the questioner is speaking, keep your eyes on him or her. Look for your references AFTER the question, not during it.

3. **Pause before beginning your answer.** Once you have heard the question, pause for approximately two seconds (*one thousand one, one thousand two*) before answering. This is a control signal. If you jump right into the answer it might seem to the audience that you haven't taken the question seriously or that you have a "pat" answer ready. Audiences are impressed with speakers who appear to think about each question just a little before answering. Now, we know that you'll probably know most answers right off the top of your head, but this is a small technique that has a big payoff for you. The extra couple of seconds will actually give you a chance to compose yourself so you can give a better answer. It's a professional approach to handling questions. If it happens that you just do not know the answer, don't be afraid to admit it. You can say, *"I don't know the answer to that question, but I'll find out and get back to you as soon as possible."* It's far better to admit that you don't know than to try to bluff your way through the answer. The audience knows when you're bluffing.

4. **Repeat questions.** When it comes to audience reaction, nothing is more frustrating to an audience than to feel left out. And they will feel left out if they can't hear the questions you're being asked. So it's your responsibility to repeat or paraphrase the question before you begin your answer. You might say something like, *"The question is, when do we plan to offer a new product line."* Then you begin your answer. In a smaller, more intimate meeting you might say, *"Victor wants to know why we don't offer free sample kits to new homeowners in the neighborhood."* You set up the answer based on the assumption that someone in the audience did not hear the question.

5. **Don't judge the questioner.** This is a tough one because human beings have a tendency to be judgmental about one another. As soon as you decide that someone isn't smart enough or interesting enough, or clever enough, or on the other hand, too smart, you've set yourself up for a fall. **You must treat every questioner as the one with the best question of the session.** You don't want to say something like, *"I think I covered that in the presentation, didn't I?"* That's condescending. Audiences are very smart. They know *immediately* when a speaker has judged a questioner. Once that happens, they become suspicious, so

why put yourself in that position when handling your q & a sessions? Do your best to remain neutral about the people asking the questions.

6. **Don't judge the question.** Here is another time when judgment calls are risky. You don't want to say something like, *"Oh, that's an excellent question."* Why not? Because the very next person ready with a question might think his or her question is less than excellent, and won't ask it. When you rate or judge a question, you're saying, in a sense, that you like some questions more than others. You want to welcome all legitimate questions. Using a rating system doesn't work in a q & a session.

7. **Include everyone as you answer.** Think of each question as one that everyone in the audience would have asked if given the chance. If you think of questions from that perspective, you'll be more inclined to use the four-second eye contact method we discussed earlier. The tendency, for most speakers, is to try to answer a question directly to the person who asked it, keeping full eye contact on the questioner for the whole answer. We think this is the wrong approach. We recommend sharing the answer with everyone and the only way to do that is with the eyes. Go around the room with your eyes and you'll find that you're able to maintain much more interest in the *q & a* portion of your presentation.

8. **End your answer on a new pair of eyes.** This might seem like odd advice since you want to make sure you've answered one individual's question, and it seems normal to look at that person to make sure you've satisfactorily answered him or her. Once again, this is a case of answering the whole audience, not just one person. When you reach the end of your answer be sure to find a new pair of eyes. Finish your answer with the new person. If you decide to go back to the original questioner, the odds are good that he or she will be ready with another question and then what happens is the two of you get into a "personal" dialogue and audiences hate it when that happens. Plan to finish your comments with a new pair of eyes. You'll be pleased with the liveliness of your *q & a* sessions.

9. **Keep your answers short and direct.** While the Q & A period is a wonderful time to expand on the ideas you presented in your speech, it is not the time for a brand new speech. Audiences prefer answers that are direct and to the point. If you have a study to share or some new statistics, this is a good time to mention them. Don't be too long-winded because this is the period set aside for the audience and its concerns. Honor this time. In other words, don't be tempted to tell how a watch is made when all someone asks is "What time is it?"

10. **What if no one asks a question?** This happens sometimes, doesn't it? You've made a great presentation, you're feeling good and you say, *"I'll be happy to answer any questions you have."* SILENCE! This is one of the moments that most speakers dread. What do you do? Wait. If you will be brave and wait for up to 10-15 seconds, in pure silence, someone will come to your rescue. This silence is absolutely frightening for most speakers, but it is essential that you wait. Here's why—the audience has been politely listening to you speak. No one has been asked to do anything. Now, the spotlight turns from you to the audience. For many people, asking a question is the same as public speaking and they're frightened. The other reason people are slow to ask questions is that they don't want to be first to test the waters. At this point, they don't know if you're going to be judgmental and it's a scary moment for them. However, when you stand in total silence, usually someone in the audience will feel sorry for you and come up with a question just to break the silence. Everything depends on how you answer that first question and that first questioner. If you follow these guidelines, you'll have all the questions you can handle. The Q & A session should be a good experience for everyone involved.

A great way to prepare for your question and answer sessions is to come up with a list of questions you think the audience is likely to ask. This list may not be 100 percent accurate because audiences can come up with surprising and obscure questions at times. Even if you only guess at one in five, you'll still feel better prepared if you've considered possible questions.

Work It Out

Write down five possible questions you might be asked for a speech or presentation you are developing.

1.

2.

3.

4.

5.

Public Speaking Demands Good Thinking

We've talked about the many things you must know in order to be a great speaker. If you choose to follow these ideas, we guarantee you'll be using your body parts along with your good common sense. After all, public speaking is about making judgment calls and the ability to take many ideas that don't seem to belong together and somehow make sense of them. Each time you prepare a speech you have created something brand new.

Public speaking demands good thinking. We know that thinking is the hardest thing we do, so it's no wonder so many people find speaking difficult. Now you know that it takes a long, long time to put together a fine presentation. This is not a task for people lacking discipline. You have shown great discipline by staying with us this long. We know you are serious about your role as a public speaker. It is an awesome task. When you get up to speak, your audience has every right to expect to hear your very best thoughts.

6.11 The Checkup: Critiquing The Speech

One of the things we recommend you do is critique every speech you give. It's not always easy to do because you are so close to it and sometimes your ego will get in the way. If at all possible, plan to have someone videotape each speech or presentation you give. There is just no better instructional tool available because you will be able to see yourself as others see you. With a videotape, it's possible to see how you're doing, what you're saying and how you look. The tape doesn't lie. We use videotape in all of our sessions on public speaking and it works.

If you don't have access to a camcorder, do an audiotape of your presentation. Listen for enthusiasm, for tone of voice, for coherency of thought, for humor, for audience reaction. Listen carefully for verbal tics such as *y'know*, *okay*, *ums* and *ers*. Often, just by hearing yourself on tape, you'll be able to eliminate these distracting mannerisms.

Be hard on yourself. When you're doing an evaluation of your speech, you want to be totally honest. During the speech, you are in the heat of the moment. After the speech, you must be cool and objective.

Ask yourself these questions:

1. What really worked well?
2. What might I have done better?
3. Did I cover all my points?
4. Was the audience attentive and with me?
5. How did the anecdotes work? Do I need new ones to make the point better?
6. Was my voice strong?
7. Did I use the 4-Second Eye Contact rule?
8. What do I need to do to make the next speech/presentation better?
9. Did I finish on time?
10. Did I use my body parts effectively?
11. Did I have fun?

It's also a great idea to ask someone to evaluate your performance. We really believe in the value of this system because a coach can give you valuable feedback that you might otherwise never hear. We use peer coaches in our seminars and each speaker finds the review helpful and meaningful. Here's a reproduction of a form we use in our seminars. Please make copies of this for your own use.

Peer Coach Review

PRESENCE:
Initial impact:

First Impressions ___ Excellent ___ Good ___ Fair
(Clothing, posture, smile, enthusiasm, etc.)
Comments:_____

OPENING STATEMENT:
Degree of interest:

___ High impact (very interesting)   ___ Low interest (ho-hum)
Comments:_____

EYE CONTACT:
Use of 4-Second Method:

___ Began with key target   ___ Did not
___ Established eye contact quickly   ___ Did not
___ Made eye contact with everyone   ___ Did not
Comments:_____

HANDS:
How did hands work?

___ Used effectively   ___ Distracting gestures
___ Hands in pockets   ___ Limited gestures
Comments:_____

ORGANIZATION:
Did presentation work?   ___ Yes   ___ No
___Appeared well prepared   ___ Presentation unfocused

OVERALL IMPACT:
10___ 9___ 8___ 7___ 6___ 5___ Other_____

Half Step

The Half Step: You

"When you have confidence, you can have a lot of fun. And when you have fun, you can do amazing things."

—Joe Namath

Half Step

The Half Step: You

Passion: Your Soul in the Presentation

What do we mean when we say *soul*? Is soul an appropriate topic to talk about in a book on public speaking? You may be asking that question as you read this. We believe that soul is the essence of the speech. It is YOU—the real you. Without this extra-added energy, you might as well forget about speaking in public.

The best speakers are those who are willing to tell their own truth, whatever that is. Anyone can get up and make a credible speech, spewing out facts and figures and using an anecdote or two to make a point. And many people do just that. Speakers who really *care* about audiences are the ones who leave a little bit of themselves with the audience each time they speak.

Great speakers know that public speaking is sharing their own individual and unique thoughts and insights. They understand that speaking from the soul requires something more than words and gestures—it requires guts. To tell your personal truth is awesome. Audiences love speakers who reveal themselves, and that's what speaking from the soul allows you to do.

How do you know when you're speaking with soul? Usually, it comes without warning. Suddenly, as you're speaking, the *sharing* of an idea becomes as important as the idea itself. You find that you have an overwhelming desire to connect with the audience. You almost miraculously find just the right words to get your message across.

Many speakers tell us that when they are speaking with soul, thirty minutes seems like one second. Time itself is transcended and although the professional speaker always finishes on time, it seems that the clock itself is no longer a barrier to communication. This type of phenomenon is called *flow*, based on the work of Mihaly Csikszentmihalyi of The University of Chicago, His best-selling book on this subject is called **Flow, The Psychology of Optimal Experience**.

He says when you experience flow, you are totally focused in the moment, and everything else fades into the background. Your energy is directed and you become one with the present. If you've ever experienced it in sports or when you're deep into a project or hobby, you know the feeling. The same experience is possible when you are up there speaking.

Can you prepare a speech with soul in mind? Yes and No. The essence of speaking from the soul implies that you have chosen to let go of your own ego for the good of the message. That is, you can choose to let go of your stage fright or nervousness, your fear of audience reaction, and you can choose to go for your own personal "gold"—the perfect 10. Now, you may not always make a perfect ten on a speech, but once you choose to make the connection of ideas more important than your personal ego, you are well on your way to speaking from your soul.

However, we know that speaking from the soul doesn't happen every time. Sometimes, the situation itself prevents you from making a great connection. Sometimes the audience just isn't ready to hear your ideas. And sometimes, you're not quite as well prepared as you'd like to be.

Always remember, you'll have another opportunity. **Never decide to give up and become an average speaker.** Know that you have an innate talent. Each time you get up to speak, you get one more chance to share your unique ideas and to touch someone.

For speakers who have experienced the phenomenon of making a true connection, it's a natural high and one they like to repeat again and again. It takes courage to do this kind of speaking because you have to allow yourself to be vulnerable instead of safe. For speakers who have not yet allowed themselves to find this place, it's an idea to think about.

You might think speaking from the soul seems contradictory to the step-by-step approach we've been offering in the pages of this book, but it's not. We're giving you the basic techniques and steps you need to know to be able to reach the soul level. Without following these steps, you won't feel comfortable enough to speak from the depth of your being.

Learn the steps, practice them, and begin to get a feel for what works and what doesn't for you, personally. This is the critical half step that will make the difference for you.

One day, as you're up there speaking, a feeling will come over you that's almost indescribable. You'll know you are speaking at a different level and you'll feel the power of your words and actions. You'll see signs of recognition in the faces of the audience, and you'll fly through the rest of your speech knowing that you've touched your own soul. When you are able to do this, you'll be touching the souls of your audience. Your body parts will be working. You'll be enjoying yourself. Congratulations you're a speaker!

Frequently Asked Questions

Here are some questions we're often asked in our Confidence Builders Presentation Skills Seminars. We're heading into the final stretch and you might have some of these same concerns. Here they are:

Isn't it true that some people are just natural born speakers?

Of course some people love speaking so much, they seem to be born to it. We know, however, that anyone can be a great speaker with the right amount of training and practice. We've seen mediocre speakers become great right in front of our eyes. All they needed was a little push in the right direction.

Do I dare to be different?

Yes, absolutely, if that fits your personal style. Some of the best speakers we know go out of their way to be wild and do things that the average speaker would never consider. These speakers make quite an impression. A caution for new speakers—being different or outrageous reminds us of the clowns you see at the Ice Capades. They take giant falls and do crazy things on the ice. They are *expert* ice skaters first and clowns second! Be an expert speaker first and do the outrageous stuff second. You'll know when you're ready.

A Couple of Examples

There's a speaker named Michael Kami. Michael speaks on Strategic Planning. His presentations are filled with unusual moves and antics. For example, he'll get down on his knee to "beg" a company president to do a Planning Gap Analysis. Michael uses humor and makes outrageous demands of his audience. And they love it! Michael has been known to hold four-day seminars on his yacht. Participants learn complicated planning concepts while sipping champagne as the yacht skims across the waters off the South Florida coastline.

Everyone knows about the super best-selling book **Chicken Soup for the Soul**. One of the co-authors, Mark Victor Hansen is one of this country's most dynamic speakers. He makes an immediate impression because he likes to wear electric blue suits. The color of his suit is like no other business suit you've ever seen. It matches his very, very blue eyes. Do you think he primes his audiences to be ready to hear him speak? You bet he does. From the moment he sprints onto the stage, everyone in the audience knows it's going to be a special experience—and Mark Victor Hansen delivers.

Les Brown became well known as a professional speaker through his series on PBS stations. Les Brown has a huge and infectious laugh that captivates his audiences. The laugh itself has become his signature. Audiences love it and expect it every time he speaks and they are never disappointed.

Why does it take so much time to create a speech?

It takes a lot of time to design and develop a good speech because of the planning and rehearsing involved. Remember our one hour per minute preparation rule. If someone else writes your speech, the time is obviously going to be drastically reduced. This is why so many executives hire speechwriters. They use them to come up with the words themselves, but also to do the research required and to develop the visual aspects of the speech. You can see that these are time consuming parts of the 6 1/2 Step process. We still like to recommend that you develop the words yourself.

What should I do if I lose my place while I'm speaking?

Don't panic! Losing your place will not destroy the speech if you stay calm when it happens. You need to take a deep breath, look at your key idea outline, and then go on. During this couple of seconds (that's all it is, not minutes), do not talk. Remember no eyes, no talk. Just look at your notes *in silence* and find your place. The audience is very forgiving when someone loses his or her place so long as the speaker does not start shaking or begin to make excuses or start leafing through piles of notes, praying to find the right place. Don't forget—the audience has no idea where you're going with the speech. Trust yourself to know that you'll recover. If you use the key idea outline method, losing your place will not be as traumatic as when you have a prepared, line for line script. Another great reason for the key idea outline.

Why do I feel so out of control every time I speak?

All of our studies point to one fact when you panic as you stand up there. *You have not prepared enough* to enter your comfort zone. For some people, the comfort zone is easy to find, for others, it takes an enormous amount of preparation to reach that state of knowing, for sure, that you know what you're doing. You'll know it when it comes. It's a feeling that comes over you that says, in effect, "No one can get to me. I know this material cold and I know I know it." When that feeling enters your consciousness, you are ready. Until then, you'll sense a little bit (or a lot) of discomfort. Keep on working on the speech until you sense the comfort. It'll be obvious when it comes. Relax and know you will be in total control on the day of the speech. This does not mean that you will not feel nervousness on the day of the speech. You will. You're supposed to feel it. It's the adrenaline pumping, getting you ready. If you don't feel these moments of nervousness, you are probably going to give a mediocre speech.

How do I create a really great opening?

We talk about creating a "grabber" for the opening. This means that the words and actions you choose should be out of the ordinary. You want to grab audience attention right away. You do this by saying or doing something unexpected and interesting. You might want to show a product demonstration, or hand out candy bars, or have special messages pasted onto the bottom of chairs that will get the audience up and active. There are as many ways to open a speech as there are speeches. This is the time to be creative.

Why not do an Ideamap about what you can do or say as you open the presentation? You might come up with a wonderful idea that will set you apart from other speakers. Be sure that whatever you choose to say or do fits in with your personality. You don't want to do something silly if you're just not the silly type. You may not want to show up with a clown nose on if that doesn't fit your personality. If it does, by all means use it. Don't be afraid to do things that are different.

Audiences love it when a speaker opens with something that is memorable and unique. All it takes is some creativity. We're not suggesting that only wild ideas work. No, all sorts of ideas work if they are *unexpected.* That's the key: do or say the unexpected and you'll get the audience to sit up and listen. For example, Jessica holds up the baby doll we've told you about and says, "Life is about communicating. Babies know it." And then she squeezes the doll's tummy and it cries and coos. Business audiences just love this little bit of fun right at the beginning of the speech. They know they're in for an interesting time—right from the opening "grabber."

What if I just can't tell a joke?

Don't worry about it. Some people can tell jokes and some people can't. If you're one who doesn't get a laugh when you tell a joke or who messes up the punch line, try other forms of humor. Your best bet will be to tell a humorous story that relates to the subject of the speech. You can weave stories into the body of the presentation easily and the laughter will come naturally from the story itself. We recommend developing a couple of good, funny stories as part of your repertoire. Use them whenever you need to add a light touch to the presentation. Know that telling a joke is an art form. Very few people have the split-second timing required to pull off a joke. Your comfort zone is more important than a joke or two.

Shouldn't I memorize my speech?

We believe that people should do what feels best and right for them concerning public speaking. Having said that, we don't like memorized speeches for *most* people. The emphasis is on the word *most*. It is clear to us that most people who make presentations are doing it for business reasons. They've been asked to speak at a national convention or they are called upon to give reports of one kind or another. This speaking is *in addition* to the regular work they do. They are not professional speakers, they are professional managers or doctors or accountants or product managers. If this is the case for you, trying to memorize a speech can be daunting at the very least and frightening at the worst. We recommend that you use our key idea outline and make your speech extemporaneous rather than memorized. We're sure you'll deliver a fine speech and get the results you want and need.

What should I do when people in the audience seem bored?

Audiences will show you how they feel about your speech. If they start fidgeting, talking, or reading, you'll know they are bored or losing interest. What can you do to get them back on track with you? Make sure your voice modulation changes often. The worst thing you can do is to speak in a monotone voice. You need to be aware of how your voice affects the audience's ability to listen. If you've been droning on for a while, shout. If you've been speaking in a loud voice, whisper. If you've been talking about light topics, tell a sad or tragic anecdote. Remember, we recommended this powerful sentence to get an audience back on track: *"Now I'm going to tell you a story."* It works every time because people love life's little stories. Of course, you have to have an arsenal of stories.

Another thing you can do to recapture a bored audience is to have them do something. Ask them to get up and stretch. Or give an unannounced break. You can have them talk with one another for a moment or two about the subject you're discussing. You must take an action of some kind to relieve the boredom. If you don't the audience will be harder and harder to reach. By the time you reach the end of your speech, you'll be exhausted and the audience will be eager to leave. This is not what you want for your speeches. The first step is to be aware of the audience and the next step is to respond appropriately.

What's the one thing I can do to increase my comfort zone?

We'll give you our most important piece of advice, plan in advance to **enjoy** the speaking event, whatever it is. If you do this, you'll experience your own comfort zone because once you decide that the speaking engagement will be a wonderful experience for you and your audience, worries and fears slip away. They'll be replaced by eagerness and enthusiasm. We told this to one of our clients and he said this one idea changed his whole attitude about speaking in public. He said he realized that he had been thinking about his presentations as hard, and something to be gotten through. Once he realized that he could enjoy the process, he became a better speaker. Before every presentation, tell yourself you're going to enjoy it and watch what happens.

What do I have to do to get a standing ovation?

A standing ovation is a special gift an audience gives to a speaker. In order to get one, you have to touch the heart and soul of each member of the audience. It's a magical chemistry that happens every once in a while. Our advice is, don't go for the standing O. Instead, make sure that every time you speak, you give your absolute best. Know that most of the time you will not receive a standing ovation unless you have celebrity status. Also know that when it happens, it's the most wonderful feeling in the world. It means that you've made just the right connection at that moment in time. Savor those moments and tuck them away in your memory bank because a true standing ovation is precious and rare. And it should be.

How to Continue

Please let us know how you're doing with your presentations and speeches. We would love to help change the world of public speaking from mediocre to great. You are going to be one of the great ones. We hope you've laughed a little and learned a lot. It's up to you now. Practice. Practice. Practice. And then, we urge you to take the extra half step—it's a short one.

How to Stay in Touch With Us

Dorothy Lynn & Jessica Selasky
Confidence Builders International, Inc.
924 SW 9th Street Circle, 206
Boca Raton, Florida 33486

561-347-1620
Fax 561-347-9701

Email: Dorolynn @AOL.com
Jselasky @AOL.com

Please visit our website: **www.confidencebuilders.com**

Thank you. Keep in touch and don't forget to have fun with your body parts every time you speak.

Index

12 most persuasive words 52
1932 World Series 123
20 hours to get ready for a 20-minute speech 11
20 hours to prepare a 20-minute speech 102
3 X 5 cards 49
4-Second Eye Contact rule 165
6 1/2 Step ANATOMY 100
6 1/2 Step Process 173
6 1/2 Step Training System 16
7 seconds 98, 154

A

acting 10
actors 115
ad lib 33, 34
Ad Libbing 33
adrenaline 10–11, 135
afraid 8, 12, 25
Albritton, Robin 96
alcohol 128
anecdote 48, 64, 66–69, 76, 97, 99, 101–102, 105–106, 125–126, 165
applause 159
Argentina 77
Attitude 155, 158
audacity 55
audience 8, 11–13, 24–29, 33, 49, 53–54, 56, 58–59, 69, 83–84, 86, 89, 93, 101, 104, 115, 119–120, 124, 128, 136, 148–149, 156, 158–159, 161, 163, 173, 175
audience analysis 30
audience confidence 31

B

Bartlett's Familiar Quotations 55
be prepared 118
Be yourself 133
Bennett, Tony 109
body language 51, 105
body part 19, 59
body parts 7, 15–16, 20, 115, 165
bored 54, 175
boredom factor 51
boring 54, 121
brain 16, 19–20, 35, 39, 44
Brain, The 44
Breathing 156
Brown, Les 152, 173

Bush, George 121
butterflies 119, 128, 135–137
Buzan, Tony 35, 39, 41
Byrd, John 87

C

camcorder 78, 116, 153, 165
canned 116
casual 150
catering department 110
Chicken Soup for the Soul 172
Churchill, Winston 132
classroom style 104
Clinton, Bill 122
close 58
closing 54, 57, 59–60, 62, 98, 101, 115, 119
Clothing 154
Clustering 38
comfort 138
comfort zone 48, 86, 173, 176
comfortable 89, 102, 104, 108, 150, 170
Computer generated presentations 86
confidence 7, 10, 131
Corpus Callosum 36
cortex 36
Creating Speeches 38
critique 165
Csikszentmihalyi, Mihaly 169
Curie, Marie 8

D

decision maker 50
deep breaths 135
Delta Airlines' Sky Magazine 87
Demosthenes 132
Develop A Speech 20
Dewey, John 55
Did I Ever Tell You About the Time 66
drink 128
Dyer, Dr. Wayne 94

E

eat 127, 158
Eating Right For High Energy 127
Edison, Thomas 16
edit 68–69
editing 99, 101, 131
Einstein, Albert 36
Emerson, Ralph Waldo 9, 13, 120

Emotional Intelligence 74
energetic 51
energy 150, 169
enjoy 10
enthousiasmos 119
enthusiasm 119–122
enthusiastic 51, 116, 119–122
excuse thinking 128
extemporaneous speaking 33, 93
eye contact 50, 58, 97, 105, 141–148, 151, 159–160
eyes 13

F

fear 7–11, 15, 25, 47–48, 135
FEAR SCALE 9
Fields, W.C. 74
fig leaf 148
Final Edit 97, 99
Final Purpose Statement 23–26, 41, 58
Fingers 47
first grader 40
first thought idea 20–21
flip chart 82–84, 104, 110
Flow, The Psychology of Optimal Experience 169
focal point 139
Folders 48
Ford, Henry 155
Fosdick, Dr. Harry Emerson 122
Four-Second Eye Contact 144
Franklin, Ben 9
Frost, Robert 55, 64–65
full-length script 59
fun 15
funny 72–74, 149

G

General Purpose Statement 20–21, 24
gestures 149, 150
Goleman, Daniel 74
Gordy, Charles 75
Gove, Bill 66
grabber 53, 57, 139, 174
Grabbers 56
Great Communicators 133

H

half step 171
Handouts 48, 89–91, 101

Hands 89, 148–150
Hansen, Mark Victor 172–173
having fun with your body parts 121
heart 59
Heraclitus 55
Hill, Napoleon 16
hotel 110
house 40
humor 14, 53, 69–72, 74–75, 88, 91, 99, 101, 111, 137

I

Ideal Environment 108
Ideamap 41–42, 59, 91–92, 174
Ideamapping 20, 38–39, 42–44, 47, 90, 131
IDEAMAPPING: Using the Right/Left Brain Theory 35
If Everything is Important, Nothing is Important 25
Information Gathering 47
Internet 49, 54
interrupt 160
introductions 124

J

James, William 155
joke 53, 149, 175
joke telling 48, 69

K

Kami, Michael 172
Kennedy, John F. 131
Key Idea Outline 35, 59–60, 62, 75, 90, 94, 97–100, 115, 119, 173
key target 141
King Jr., Martin Luther 118, 132

L

Last Minute Jitters 102
laugh 73, 75, 105, 173
laughing 8, 74, 120, 141
Laughter Precedes Learning 75
lectern 11, 95, 105, 109, 159
left brain 36–38, 41, 43, 100
left brain/right brain 36
linear thinking 36
Location 103

M

magazines 49
Managing Your Mind & Mood Through Food 127
manuscript 94, 95
memorize 59, 93, 100, 118, 175
memorized 54, 93–94, 115
memory 19
Men's Health Magazine 74
microphones 109–111
Mind Map Book, The 35
Mindmapping 38–39
modulate 67
monotone 142

N

National Speakers Association 66
natural 116–117, 121–122, 152, 172
negative self talk 15
Nerves 128
nervous 15, 78, 103, 119, 127
nervousness 11, 13, 119, 136, 151
No Eyes, No Talk 84, 144, 146, 173
Note Cards 49
Now I'm going to tell you a story 67, 69, 176

O

Oak Tag 60
Olympics 123
One-Two Punch 157
Opening 52–53, 56–59, 62, 98, 101, 115, 118, 139, 151
outlining 34, 37, 47
overhead projector 84–85
Overprepare 11, 48

P

Pacing 151–152, 156
Palmer, Arnold 123
panic 93–94, 103, 111
Passion 169
Pause 58, 97, 126, 151, 157–158, 161
PBS 173
Peer Coach Review 166
PEP 124–127
personal comfort level 11
personal comfort zone 95, 110, 141
persuasive speech 52
planning 12, 19–20, 47
pockets 150
Podium 109
poise 139
Posture 151–153
preparation 119
Prepared 116, 121–122, 173
presence 139, 146, 155, 158
Presidents 121
probability thinking 27
professional speakers 7
projector 110–111
prop 56, 57
Purpose 20

Q

Q & A session 143, 162–163
question and answer session 59, 118
questions 51, 95, 159
Quick Tips 28
Quick Tips for Working with a Teleprompter 97
quotation 55, 57
Quotations 48

R

ramble 51, 159
Read 94–95
Reader's Digest 55
Reagan, Ronald 121
rehearsal 69, 86, 115–116, 119
rehearse 60, 97, 115, 119
rehearsing 12, 131
Reilly, Charles 33, 117
Relationship Speaking 66
research 47
Respect 138
Restek, Richard 44
reverse fig leaf 148
right brain 37, 42–43
right brained 34
Road Not Taken, The 64
Robbins, Anthony 152
Robinson, Grady Jim 66
rocker 153
Roman Numeral Outlining 34, 37, 43–44, 59
Roosevelt, Eleanor 10, 132
rough draft 68–69, 97
round tables 106
Ruth, Babe 123

S

scared 19
script 97, 100
scripted 149
seating arrangements 104
self-confidence 15, 69
Self-Introductions 126
shouting 142
Show and Tell 89
Signals of Communication 56, 62, 88
SILENCE 163, 173
sit 109
smile 10, 51, 59–60, 71, 74, 97–98, 108, 120, 126
smiling 74, 105, 120, 156
so that Formula 20–24, 26, 32, 41, 53, 98, 101
soul 120, 169–171, 176
South Florida Women's Business Conference 108
speak extemporaneously 33–34, 59, 134
Speak louder 51
Speak Louder or Softer 142
speaking anxiety 47
Speaking Extemporaneously 33
speaking signature 94
speaking temperature 7
Speech 101 143
speechwriters 94, 173
spelling 83
Spidering 38
stage 12–13, 104
stage presence 152
standing ovation 19, 105, 110, 176
standing up 8
startling statistic 11, 51, 56, 57, 58, 81
Statistics 48
Stomach 67
stories 55, 64–69, 71–72, 76, 78, 108, 175
surefire idea 67
Swayer, The 152
Synergy 37

T

Take Your Pulse 13, 14
T-Bar 27–31, 33, 48, 98
T-Bar Analysis 20, 25–26, 29, 31, 32, 101
Teleprompter 96
tell you a story 67, 69, 176
Thank You 58
theater style 105
three key ideas 27
tie-up statement 58
Tips for Editing Your Speech 100
Titles 91–92, 126
Touch, Turn, Talk 84
Transparencies 84–85
trigger 62
Twain, Mark 70, 138
two-minute profile 76, 78

U

uh 144, 146
um 144, 146
unfounded fear 10
Use Both Sides of Your Brain 39
U-Shape 105

V

videos 88
videotaping 110
Vignettes 48, 55, 66–68
visual aids 47–48, 51, 56, 76, 81–83, 86–87, 89, 91, 98–99, 101–102, 116, 119
Visualization 122–123
visualize 37
visuals 12

W

Webbing 38
What Are You Looking At? 96
whispering 142
Williams, Robin 33
Wilson, Woodrow 99
Work It Out 10, 13, 23, 32, 39, 41, 57, 68, 73, 76, 92, 98, 126, 133, 147, 149, 164
Write 53, 69, 84, 118
writing 44
Wurtman, Dr. Judith 127–128

Y

Yale University's Psychology Department 52
yawning 50–51, 141
Yeats, William Butler 131
You'll See It When You Believe It 94

Z

Ziglar, Zig 152
zone 156

Order Form

Telephone orders: Call Toll Free: 1-877-333-8876. Have your Visa or MasterCard ready.

Fax orders: (513) 336-9159

Mail orders: Funny Management Publishing, 924 SW 9th Street Circle, #206, Boca Raton, FL 33486

Please send the following books and/or tapes:

		Quantity	Total
☐ Book: Your Public Speaking Workout	@ 14.95	_____	_____
☐ Audio Tape: 6 1/2 Steps to Speaking Success	@ 10.00	_____	_____
☐ Audio Tape: 6 1/2 Steps to Writing Success	@ 10.00	_____	_____
☐ Audio Tape: 6 1/2 Steps to Listening Success	@ 10.00	_____	_____
☐ Boxed set of all 3 audio tapes	@ 25.00	_____	_____

Company Name:_____

Name: _____

Address:_____

City:_____ State:_____ Zip:_____

Form of payment:
☐ Check
☐ Credit Card ___Visa ___MasterCard

Card Number:_____

Name on Card:_____

Expiration Date:_____

Shipping: Book rate $3.00 for first book and $1.00 for each additional book. Tapes $2.00 for one tape and $3.00 for boxed set. Call for overnight rates 1-877-333-8876.

Call Dorothy or Jessica at Confidence Builders for information about workshops, seminars, and keynote speeches. Call toll free at 1-877-333-8876 or visit our Web site at www.confidencebuilders.com.

Confidence Builders International, Inc.
Mission Statement

WE FOCUS ON FUN! WE CREATE ABUNDANCE!
Confidence Builders designs and delivers the highest quality management development programs, services & products. Our motto, *Laughter Precedes Learning*, creates success for everyone involved with us.